A PLUME BOOK

HIGH POINTS AND LOWS

Born and raised in High Point, North Carolina, AUSTIN CARTY first came to notice in 2006 as a popular contestant on the TV show *Survivor: Panama—Exile Island*. He has since become a widely sought after inspirational speaker, addressing audiences young and old, Christian and secular. *High Points and Lows* is his first book of nonfiction.

Praise for Austin Carty and *High Points and Lows*

"Reading *High Points and Lows* left me thinking, 'Isn't it nice to learn from others?' It sure is! And you will learn, laugh, wonder, and thank God for life as you read Austin Carty's stories. With each story I found him connecting with my heart and challenging me to be different. What a gift."   —Doug Fields, Saddleback Church

"This is a fun book to read, in addition to all it says about the struggles and joys that accompany growing up in Christ. I'm going to get my college-age grandchild to read it. It's that good!"
           —Tony Campolo, bestselling author of
                         Letters to a Young Evangelical

"These charming essays possess memoirs' most important quality: lack of inhibition. In *High Points and Lows*, Austin Carty invites readers to share his most intimate misadventures in faith, doubt, television celebrity, and Southern American coming-of-age. This collection is a generous gift to readers of all backgrounds and beliefs, imbued with wonder, compassion, playfulness, pop culture, and self-deprecation. If St. Augustine watched cable television and drove a Dodge pickup, one wonders if *The Confessions* wouldn't read like this."   —Koren Zailckas, author of *Smashed: Story of a Drunken Girlhood*

"*High Points and Lows* is deceptive: Carty lures you in with his easy wit and entertaining stories, but then he nudges you into a deeper truth about Jesus and faith. If youth and singles pastors could make the gospel as relatable as Carty has, I suspect there'd be a lot more butts in the pews."   —Susan E. Isaacs, author of
                         Angry Conversations with God

"Austin Carty has a gift unique in Christian circles: he's refreshingly honest, genuinely funny, and uncommonly humble. Here is the life of a believer—mountaintops, valleys, and the occasional desert island. Christian colleges would do well by making this book required reading for every freshman class. Faith is messy because life is messy. But it's a beautiful mess."

—Cathleen Falsani, author of *Sin Boldly:*
A Field Guide for Grace and *The Dude Abides:*
The Gospel According to the Coen Brothers

"I'm not sure if Jesus sat in a rocking chair drinking sweet tea as he talked theology, but maybe the Pharisees would have loosened up a little if he had. *High Points and Lows* is sweet tea theology, down home Southern style, and whether you are a small-town carpenter or a Southern Baptist preacher, you'll find a little something of God in here. No doubt, Austin's story will help many a lonely hitchhiker thumb their way to heaven."

—Shane Claiborne, author of *Jesus for*
President and founder of the Simple Way

"From Bayside High to Beyoncé, Austin Carty leaves no pop culture stone unturned in this valuable book about the nature of family, the complexities of Christian faith, and the minor tragedies of teenage life. It's funny, irreverent, and wise. If Carty ever starts his own denomination, I am so there."

—Kevin Roose, author of *The Unlikely Disciple:*
A Sinner's Semester at America's Holiest University

"Authentic. That's the word, authentic. Austin Carty tells the truth in his charming and disarming new book. He tells the truth in anecdotes about himself, which is probably why his telling the truth about us, the church, is illuminating."

—Dan Merchant, filmmaker and author of
Lord, Save Us from Your Followers

HIGH POINTS AND LOWS

✳ ✳ ✳

Life, Faith, and Figuring It All Out

Austin Carty

A PLUME BOOK

PLUME
Published by the Penguin Group
Penguin Group (USA) Inc., 375 Hudson Street, New York, New York 10014, U.S.A.
Penguin Group (Canada), 90 Eglinton Avenue East, Suite 700, Toronto, Ontario,
Canada M4P 2Y3 (a division of Pearson Penguin Canada Inc.)
Penguin Books Ltd., 80 Strand, London WC2R 0RL, England
Penguin Ireland, 25 St. Stephen's Green, Dublin 2, Ireland
(a division of Penguin Books Ltd.)
Penguin Group (Australia), 250 Camberwell Road, Camberwell, Victoria 3124,
Australia (a division of Pearson Australia Group Pty. Ltd.)
Penguin Books India Pvt. Ltd., 11 Community Centre, Panchsheel Park,
New Delhi – 110 017, India
Penguin Group (NZ), 67 Apollo Drive, Rosedale, North Shore 0632, New Zealand
(a division of Pearson New Zealand Ltd.)
Penguin Books (South Africa) (Pty.) Ltd., 24 Sturdee Avenue, Rosebank,
Johannesburg 2196, South Africa

Penguin Books Ltd., Registered Offices: 80 Strand, London WC2R 0RL, England

First published by Plume, a member of Penguin Group (USA) Inc.

First Printing, February 2010
10 9 8 7 6 5 4 3

Copyright © Austin Carty, 2010
All rights reserved

A section of "Man-to-Man Chats" originally appeared in slightly different form in
Charisma.

Ⓟ REGISTERED TRADEMARK—MARCA REGISTRADA

LIBRARY OF CONGRESS CATALOGING-IN-PUBLICATION DATA
Carty, Austin.
  High points and lows : life, faith, and figuring it all out / Austin Carty.
    p. cm.
  ISBN 978-0-452-29580-3
  1. Carty, Austin. 2. Christian biography. I. Title.
  BR1725.C36A3 2010
  277.3'083092—dc22
  [B]
                                                              2009024114

Printed in the United States of America
Set in Sabon
Designed by Leonard Telesca

Penguin is committed to publishing works of quality and integrity.
In that spirit, we are proud to offer this book to our readers;
however, the story, the experiences, and the words
are the author's alone.

For my dad, Seadog, who was always man enough
to tell me he loved me

Contents

Whether there was anything but imagination in the faith, or anything but egoism in the love, God knows. I don't.

—C. S. Lewis

Coke on the Rocks

B ack when I used to drink more than I do today, I loved beer and whiskey. Something about Jack Daniel's, with its south-of-the-Mason-Dixon-Line bottle and classic black-and-white label, made me feel nostalgic: I think it was a false sense of Southern pride, as though drinking Jack somehow supported an argument that our side actually won the Civil War. On the other hand, beer screamed masculinity. It told the world that I was from humble roots, that I was lower than the rich folks who drank martinis and gin, and proud not to be one of them.

The catch is that I was never really a big drinker. Sure, I tried to party hard, tried to be a rebel, but it just didn't take. I was too soft, too polished, too nice and caring. I didn't want to get plastered and say rude things to people, and I never got drunk enough to think I could beat up guys three times my size. Still, like the little engine that could, I would be at a party three to four nights a week, beer or whiskey in hand, toasting to Lord only knows what.

But there were also times when I would go through spiritual peaks—times when I'd be riding Jesus highs and want to display my love for God's Son by no longer drinking. During these fleeting spurts of religiosity there was nothing I'd love more than hanging out at a party or bar without a beer or whiskey in hand. I wanted everyone to ask me why I wasn't drinking so I could answer, in an oh-so-condescending way, "Because I'm a Christian."

It took me years to realize that I wasn't abstaining from drinking because I desperately wanted to please God; instead I desperately wanted for people to say, "Austin's a good Christian." In other words, for the first quarter century of my life I went through the motions of religiosity in hopes that people would think me a good guy. And what I'm ashamed to admit is that I was foolish enough to think this made any difference to God.

I still frequently find myself in places where alcohol is being served, and I remember how I used to think of them as battlefields where I could make heroic Christian stands. In days past, when I would make a show of not drinking, I'd sometimes hold a glass of water in my hand, raising it every few seconds to my lips just so everyone could see that I was only drinking water. Now on nights when I don't feel like having a drink, I'll order a Coke instead of water, but I'll ask for it to be served in a high-ball glass, "on the rocks."

The one remarkable truth about Christianity is that it's all a matter of the heart. You can avoid curse words your whole life, bake brownies every day for bake sales, lead prayer meetings at your house, never touch alcohol, never have premarital sex, and still, if it isn't because you really believe that Jesus is still alive and you love him for it, you're wasting your time. That is the beauty of the Christian religion, and also the rub. Only each individual can determine whether he's committed, abstaining, practicing, etc. for the real reason.

In days past, my ultimate faith high would come from hearing that someone thought I was a "good Christian." This would excite me for a few seconds, but then I would feel as if I needed to hear it from someone else, because in truth what I really needed was to prove to *myself* that I was a good Christian. What I have finally discovered is very simple: the opinions of others don't satisfy my faith. Instead, it is my assurance that I know Jesus that gives me the peace I crave.

Trust me, I still love to discuss faith. But these days I'm determined not to flaunt it, because the moment I do my faith becomes a crutch, a social club, a membership

I maintain in order to feel that my life is important. That's why, until the topic materializes of its own accord, I bide my time with a highball glass in hand, laughing and forming friendships with people who don't necessarily believe the same things I do. And when my drink runs low I mosey over and get the barkeep's attention. When he asks me what I want, I smile and tell him: "Coke on the rocks."

More than a Number

"Now, for the ultimate test of whether or not you are saved," said the famous evangelist.

My heart was racing as I awaited the Jesus litmus test, a test I had apparently gone eighteen years as a Christian without taking or even being aware of. I was petrified. *What if I'm* not *saved*, I suddenly thought. Is it possible that all this time I've been deluding myself? How could there be a simple test for this that I *don't* know about?

My legs were trembling, and so was my entire faith foundation, something I had considered rock solid before Famous Evangelist showed up. I was looking on with fear and anticipation, eagerly awaiting his next words. But instead of continuing, Famous Evangelist paused. He waited for what seemed like an eternity, building suspense.

Famous Evangelist—who incidentally looked exactly like Don Flamenco from the video game *Mike Tyson's Punch-Out!!*—was the featured speaker at my Christian college's Spiritual Emphasis Week during my freshman year. Now, ten years later, I remember how deftly he employed his oratorical skill, and the way he balanced humor and pathos. Just before beginning his first speech, he told us that he had come straight from an event at a college up north. At that event, he said, 362 people had been saved. He quickly emphasized that he hadn't told us that figure in order to brag, but rather to demonstrate the power of God. I didn't care why he told us he'd saved 362 people; I just wondered how he knew it was 362. This seemed to me an impossibly difficult and specific number to come by.

In one of his speeches, Famous Evangelist told us all about his baby son, relating touching anecdotes about the boy's birth and his first steps, about his first illness and his love for his daddy. Then Famous Evangelist told us about how much God loved *his* Son, the man we knew as Jesus, and he explained to us how much it hurt God to sacrifice his Son. Suddenly, all the lights in the gymnasium went out and music boomed overhead, kind of like when the Jordan-era Bulls announced its starting lineup. Then a screen fell from the sky and images began appearing. They were images of Famous Evangelist's son: pictures of the young boy in Halloween outfits, of him with chocolate smeared across his cheeks, of him holding his daddy's hand at the edge of the ocean. The next thing we knew, Famous Evangelist was crying. He was telling us how much he loved *his* son, how he loved him too much to sacrifice him, how he couldn't fathom the depth of God's love because he, himself, wouldn't be able to make the same sacrifice that God did.

Now, Famous Evangelist was arguably the most gifted speaker I've ever heard, which explains why I was waiting with such rapt attention for him to tell me how to take the salvation test. Looking back on it, I think I imagined that this test would be something practical, like peeing on a plastic stick and waiting to see whether it came up pink or blue.

"The ultimate test," he finally said, "is this: are you keeping his commandments?"

Famous Evangelist slowly paced back and forth across the stage, sighing into the microphone. "Jesus tells us that *this* is the only indicator of whether or not we are saved. Jesus says, 'If you love me, keep my commandments.' "

He paused, scanning the entire audience. "It's pretty simple. Are you keeping his commandments, or are you living a life of sin?"

Suddenly, I felt nauseous, my stomach twisting into knots. I was thinking of the times I had gotten drunk the previous summer, of the lustful thoughts that crossed my mind each day, of the foul language I often used with my buddies. I knew that these things were not in accordance with the ways of God. So when Famous Evangelist told me that these were scriptural evidence of my *not* being saved, I felt hollow inside.

"Now," Famous Evangelist resumed, as strains of piano music began to fill the air, "I don't know where you all are in your lives. I don't know what you've been through. But I do know this: if you don't have Jesus Christ in your heart, then you have no hope for salvation."

As he continued, the music steadily grew louder. "The question is very simple. You can hear Jesus calling you. He's saying, 'I love you. Do you love *me*?'"

Famous Evangelist paused, cueing the praise leader to begin singing softly a song that spoke of surrendering to God's will.

"And there's only one way you can know if you love Jesus," Famous Evangelist picked back up, his voice carrying over the music. "And that's by keeping his commandments. If you haven't been keeping his commandments, then you don't really love him. But tonight God's giving you the chance to love him."

Again Famous Evangelist paused.

"So I'd like you all to bow your heads," he whispered.

The praise leader started singing a touch louder.

"And now, with heads bowed and eyes closed," Famous Evangelist continued, "if you believe that you have not been keeping God's commandments . . . if you feel like God is speaking to your heart right now . . . if you feel you need to be saved . . . if you want to spend eternity in heaven . . . then please raise your hand."

My chest was pounding.

"Thank you," I heard Famous Evangelist whisper. "I see your hands. God does too. Thank you."

Furtively, I peeked through my fingers, trying to gauge how many hands had been lifted. I made out a couple and then shut my eyes, hoping no one had caught me peeking.

"Several people have raised their hands," Famous Evangelist said. "Those people are making a confession of Christ. They want to be saved. Do *you* want to be saved, too? If you feel like God is tugging at your heart, just surrender. Let go. It's that easy."

Famous Evangelist stopped for a second and then added, "No one is looking. This is just between you and God. Do you feel him calling you?"

My fingers quivered as fear began working through me like a drug. I thought I was already saved, but I wanted to be sure. I mean, who *doesn't* want to be sure they're going to heaven?

Should I raise my hand? I wondered.

"Don't be scared," Famous Evangelist said. "*This* is how you can be certain that you are going to heaven. This is how you know you are saved. This is how you can have a relationship with God. Just confess your love for Christ. It's easy: just raise your hand."

It was after hearing those words that I slowly lifted my arm. It was a limp, lifeless gesture, one that signaled a profession not only of faith but also of confusion. I understood just one thing in that moment: I wanted to know for certain that I was saved. And if lifting my arm was what it took, then fine, I had no problem touching some sky.

"Thank you, thank you," Famous Evangelist kept saying as more hands lifted. "There is a joyous celebration taking place in heaven right this minute. All the angels are rejoicing for you . . . for those of you who have raised your hands."

With my head bowed, I pictured a bunch of revelers in white robes: translucent figures waving halos through the air like ravers with glow sticks; cherubs chanting my name and raising the roof.

"Praise the Lord," Famous Evangelist continued. "Thank you, Jesus."

He took a deep breath, as if to signal that he was about to begin a new line of thought.

"Now," he began, "if there are any of you who believe you *already* know Christ, but you feel that you haven't been as close to him lately as you should be and you want to grow closer to him tonight, please raise your hands."

Famous Evangelist paced for several seconds, then continued:

"Or if there are any of you who are wrestling with

some sin in your life and you'd like to draw closer to God . . . please raise *your* hands."

My arm was becoming very heavy now, seeing as it had been in the air for over five minutes. I was beginning to wonder what else Famous Evangelist could possibly ask to draw more hands: How about those of you who ate breakfast this morning? How about those of you who brushed your teeth last night?

Finally, it seemed that Famous Evangelist was comfortable with the number of raised hands. He began praying for everyone, and I thought this was going to be the end of the experience.

But then he spoke back up.

"Now there is only one other thing that Jesus wants of you. In the Bible, Jesus says that it is those who confess their faith in him with their mouths that are saved. So to show that you *really* believe in what you've just done, Jesus would like you to go one step further tonight.

"I am opening up this basketball court as an altar. Now, this is a safe place. It's a place for you to come and show your love for Jesus. Please come forward and make the profession of your faith public."

The next thing I knew, I was out of my seat and kneeling on the basketball court with nearly two hundred other students. Several people around me were crying. I heard many of them mumbling prayers. The music from overhead was coming louder than ever, and

Famous Evangelist was walking among us and addressing us all. "I am so happy for you. Lord bless you. Praise
you, Jesus. The glory is yours, Jesus."

After a minute or two of kneeling silently, I heard
footsteps behind me. I imagined it was Famous Evangelist and I wanted to sneak a quick peek at him. But when
I twisted around I found not Famous Evangelist, but
rather a man with a counting device. I saw him pointing
at my head, his lips mumbling the number eighty-seven
before glancing to the girl next to me and mumbling
eighty-eight.

When the event ended, a mass of people who had
been in the audience and seen me walk down to the altar
came running to hug me. They told me how excited they
were for me.

How do you *feel*? they all asked. Do you feel *amazing*?

And while I assured them that, yes, I felt amazing, I
knew in my heart that I was lying, that I really felt confused. I secretly wondered what had just happened. Had
this been real? Did raising my hand and walking up on
stage really solidify my trip to heaven? Why was this
any different from the first time I'd professed my belief
in Jesus? Was getting saved a second time like buying
salvation insurance? Why wasn't I crying like all those
people around me?

There was only one thing I *did* feel for certain.

I felt like a number.

• • •

Over the next year I'd learn that events like the one conducted by Famous Evangelist are very common in pop-Christian circles. There is a proven formula for these events, and it seldom varies. The formula goes (almost exactly) like this:

- A speaker offers anecdotes illustrating how "bad" he was (before God saved him from being bad).
- The speaker starts talking more slowly and more dramatically at around the forty-five minute mark (this is when piano music materializes, always seemingly from nowhere).
- The speaker tells the audience members to bow their heads and close their eyes, promising them that no one's looking (i.e., "This is just between you and God").
- The speaker asks those who would like to be Christians to raise their hands. Then, seconds later, he/she begins whispering "thank you" over and over again into the microphone (both to God and to those who've raised their hands).
- The speaker paces the stage dramatically, telling the audience that God would like them to go one step further (i.e., "Christ wants you to confess his name publicly").

- The speaker opens the altar and a crowd of people come forward (many crying, many more confused). The speaker begins walking among the people and praying for them.
- Somewhere, someone begins counting the number of people who have come forward (or at least the approximate number).
- The speaker wraps up the event with a prayer. Then a band plays emotive praise songs while everyone disperses.
- The audience members who didn't go forward walk down and fawn over those who did, expressing how happy they are for them.

Since I am somewhat cynical about Christian speakers, it is ironic that I now travel internationally in that exact role. I never intended to fall into public speaking; it just kind of happened. In college I majored in communications, but that's only because I didn't have a clue about what I wanted to do with my life. All I really wanted was to get through school doing as little work as possible, and a communications degree seemed the easiest way to make that happen. To this day I'm not sure what one *does* with a communications degree. I'm pretty sure that math and history majors communicate just as much as I do (and probably much more effectively). Anyway, my point is this: I was caught off guard when I received my first invitation to speak at an event.

I was fortunate enough to get cast on the TV show *Survivor* a couple of years ago, and the invitation came the day after I was voted off. I was being asked to speak at a trade show for the United States Postal Service and I was flattered. I said yes immediately.

A week before the show, I sat down to write the speech. Two hours later, when I closed my computer, I was shocked by what I'd learned through the speech-writing process. It seemed that nearly every thought I had regarding life, struggle, hardships, humility, love, and *Survivor* was colored by my Christian faith. But this speech was intended for a secular audience, so I tried to cut out as many overt Christian references as possible.

Still, I couldn't seem to separate my ideas about life from my ideas about faith. This made me come to terms with a simple fact: I really *do* believe the whole Jesus thing, and my faith drives my every thought.

Now, I must confess: I envisioned my U.S. Postal Service speech as a kind of oratorical clinic. I planned to open with a line that would endear me to the audience, something witty and insightful that would cause them to roar with laughter. Then I would suffocate the room with a touching story, evoking tears and empathy from my new friends. I figured that by the time I was done speaking, each member of the audience would have experienced a full range of emotions, and the U.S. Postal Service would sell enough stamps to put FedEx out of business.

Ah, the fantasies.

When my name was introduced and I stepped to the microphone, this is what came out:

"How is everyone today?"

Silence.

"Oh, come on, you can do better than that. I *said*, how *is* everyone today?!"

That's right: an intro pulled straight from the first page of *How to Give Lame Speeches for Dummies.*

Luckily, I was able to get my footing about halfway through, and overall the speech turned out okay.

Not great.

Probably not even *good.*

But okay.

I included more Christian material in the speech's actual delivery than I had in preparing the text, primarily because I am the kind of guy whose mind wanders while he's talking, and consequently I end up doing a lot of impromptu rambling. I closed the speech with a word of thanks, and then opened the floor for audience members to ask me questions about *Survivor.*

Hands shot up all around the room.

But, much to my surprise, many of the questions I fielded concerned my comments about Jesus rather than my feelings about Jeff Probst. And when I was leaving that afternoon, I had several audience members approach me, asking if I'd be willing to speak at their churches.

I remember one very nice man with a *Magnum, P.I.* mustache, who was pressing me about speaking to his daughter's youth group.

"Please," he said. "The youth pastor is having a really hard time getting through to these kids. Most of them don't even want to be at church. They just go because their parents make them."

Immediately, I pictured Famous Evangelist. I felt sick at the idea of standing in front of a group of young adults and trying to sell them salvation. Even if I believed wholeheartedly in the product, I wanted other people to buy it on their own terms.

I smiled at the man and thanked him very much for the offer. "I just don't want to turn Jesus into a stage show," I said.

The man shook his head. "You misunderstand me," he said. "I don't want you to go there trying to save souls. I just want you to do what you did here. Just talk about Jesus, tell them what you think about him, and then let the kids make up their own minds."

"I don't know," I said. "I mean, this was a speech in a convention center and to a secular crowd. What you're asking me to do would be in a church . . . to a religious crowd."

The man stroked his mustache, as if taming it. "You know, just because it's in a church doesn't mean it has to be *religious*."

As soon as he said that, it was like truth had punched me in the face. It was such a simple statement; yet because I was so accustomed to Christian speakers following the same pat formula, it never occurred to me that someone could speak, in Christian circles, *just* about Jesus.

A week later I was speaking at the man's church in central North Carolina.

A month later I was speaking at Saddleback Church in Orange County, California.

A few months after that I was speaking in the Far East.

Several years later I'm still traveling, still talking about Jesus, and still refusing to ask people to close their eyes and bow their heads.

A little over a year ago I got invited to be the headline speaker at a big Christian event in Georgia. It was one of the largest events I've ever been asked to do, and it showcased over a dozen major Christian bands. I flew into the airport a couple of hours before the event was scheduled to begin, which should have left me ample time to get to the venue. I'll spare you the details of my woes with the rental car folks, but suffice it to say that by the time

I arrived in my electric-purple Chevy Cavalier, I had less than thirty minutes to prepare.

Now, this theater was something else. It was a massive castle of a building that had Christian regalia plastered all over the outside walls (crosses, Jesus fish, Bible verses, etc.). On the inside were countless paintings of Jesus, all of which were for sale, and all of which depicted him looking very much like Billy Ray Cyrus (with the exception of one that made him look more like Kurt Cobain).

I spent about five minutes staring at one of the Billy Ray paintings (in which the mulleted Christ figure was stroking a baby lamb) before someone very official looking ushered me backstage to meet the man responsible for organizing the event (we'll call him Bob).

"We were getting worried," Bob said as we shook hands. "You ready to go on?"

"Absolutely," I said. "I'm excited to be here."

"Great. We're excited to have you. We are big *Survivor* fans at my house."

"Oh yeah?"

"Yeah. The biggest. I hope you don't mind if I ask you a bunch of questions about the show tonight after the event is over."

"Of course not."

He smiled. "Good. I have several questions I've been dying to ask. But we don't have time now. We only have a few minutes before you go on."

I glanced at my cell phone to see what time it was: 7:22.

"Eight minutes," I said.

"Okay, so we need to talk fast then. Follow me. We'll go meet Bryan. He'll be the one coming onstage to provide backing music when you give the invitation."

I went stiff. "Invitation?" I stuttered.

"Yeah, just follow me. Bryan's in the next room with the band."

I followed the man into the room, my heart racing. I recalled Famous Evangelist strutting the stage during the invitation he had given at my college, scaring me into coming forward all those years ago. I couldn't give an invitation: it would fly directly in the face of everything I would be speaking about.

I suddenly felt nauseous.

"Austin, this is Bryan," said Bob, introducing me to a skinny young guy in a weird jacket that looked like the one Cap'n Crunch wears.

"Nice to meet you," he said.

"You too."

"Now, Austin," Bob said. "How would you like this to work? What should cue Bryan to start playing the backing music?"

"Umm," I stuttered. "I . . . well, to be honest, I usually don't *do* an invitation. I typically—"

The man's face froze. "Austin," he said calmly. "This

is in your contract. You *have* to do an invitation. We *have* to have one."

I was momentarily stunned. Somehow I'd either over-looked this detail or miscommunicated with my agent.

"It will be fine," the man assured me. "Just give a quick invitation at the end of your speech. It's simple."

I stammered. "Umm, I . . ."

"Is there anything particular you would like to talk about while doing it?" Bob asked. "Maybe something that could tip Bryan off so he knows when to begin playing?"

I was beginning to sweat. I racked my brain, trying to think of how I could best negotiate the situation. I stood silently for what felt like hours.

Finally, I came up with an idea I could live with.

I looked at Bryan. "When you hear me start talking about an old Scottish man who used to be my soccer coach, you can start playing."

"Cool," Bryan said.

Five minutes later, I was on the stage. The theater was packed with approximately two thousand kids. Every single person in the audience had come with his or her church youth group, having been bused in from all over the Southeast.

Now, it should go without saying that any young adult who has come hundreds or thousands of miles to attend a Christian youth event on the weekend has, oh, about a 99 percent chance of already *being* Christian. I'm pretty sure this is precisely where they get the phrase *preaching to the choir.*

But anyway . . .

I went through my speech, telling the kids how I believe that Christianity has gotten a bad rap and how I think Jesus is so much better than "Christianity." I told them how I think it is such a blessing to really believe in someone bigger than myself, how it colors the way I see the whole world. I told them that being a Christian isn't about following a code of ethics or about going to church every weekend but is, rather, about knowing a man named Jesus and trying to live a life driven by the same kind of love and universal respect with which Jesus lived his. As usual I referenced many quotes from music and movies while trying to express my ideas.

Finally, I started wrapping up, and I could tell that I had half of the audience interested and the other half ready to take knives to their wrists.

I knew the invitation was looming, and so I began sweating again. I started walking the stage in silence, trying to organize my thoughts.

After a few moments, I began:

"When I was in college, I used to attend events like this all the time. I remember how speakers would come in and give these dynamic addresses, and then suddenly they'd get really emotional and start talking slowly into the microphone. Soon they'd ask us to bow our heads and close our eyes, promising us that no one was looking. Then they'd ask us to raise our hands if we wanted salvation.

"Now, I want you all to understand how much I believe in Christian salvation. I think it is the most beautiful thing in the world. I think it is real and it is pure and it is life changing. And there is nothing I'd like more than for those of you who don't already consider yourselves Christians to begin a relationship with Jesus.

"But, I know how tricky moments like these are.

"I've seen so many people come forward at events like this because they get scared, or because the speaker makes them feel guilty. I've seen just as many come forward because one of their friends came forward.

"Meanwhile, I've also known people who have invited Jesus into their lives at events like this, but they didn't come forward because they were too uncomfortable, or because they were embarrassed, or because they were confused. Those people were left wondering if their experience wasn't as real as everyone else's simply because they didn't come forward.

"Guys, I'm here to tell you that there *is* no formula for this. There *is* no right way to meet Jesus. As I said earlier, all being *saved* means is that you have come to believe that Jesus is real . . . that you have asked him to be a part of your life . . . that you want to be able to talk to him the way you talk to a friend.

"And this can happen anywhere and at any time."

I paused, remembering my moment with Famous Evangelist.

"You know," I began again. "I got scared into coming forward at an event like this once. Even though I was already a Christian, the speaker tricked me into believing I wasn't. And it left me confused and fearful for a long time."

I paused again, this time remembering the man who, without realizing it, taught me that the act of salvation was not intended to be a spectacle but rather was a personal thing.

"I once had this soccer coach," I said, "this sweet little man from Scotland. By the time I played for him he was in his early seventies. His name was Willie Bell and he used to coach in the English Premier League, which is the soccer equivalent to coaching basketball in the NBA.

"Now, this man had no business coaching a team like mine. He was far too qualified. But soon after my coach became a Christian, he decided he wanted to coach at a Christian college in America."

Suddenly, I heard Bryan beginning to play the piano behind me. I glanced around and saw him standing there in his Cap'n Crunch outfit, nodding at me.

"After every game we played," I continued, "our coach would ask the other team to come pray with us. Win, lose, or draw, he'd ask. And nine times out of ten, they'd come. So there we'd be, all huddled up around midfield.

"Our coach would begin talking, and he'd always tell a quick anecdote about a young man he knew only briefly, a young man who became a Christian in his presence. Our coach would tell us how the young man, a couple of months after he accepted Jesus, found out he had a tumor in his leg. He'd tell us how less than two months later, the young man—whose name was Ian—died.

"Then our coach would look at all the players and say, 'I'm going to see Ian.'

"And then he'd ask a very simple question: 'Are *you* going to see Ian?' "

I paused, making sure that I had the group's attention.

"Our coach would then say something that has stuck with me to this very day. He'd say, 'If *you'd* like to know Jesus, all you have to do is tell him. You don't have to tell me. You don't have to raise your hand or stand up. This is all a matter of the heart. You just have to really believe it. That's all you have to do.' "

I paused, looked over the audience.

"That is the same message I want to leave *you* with tonight," I said. "If you want to come forward to this altar and pray about something, then please come forward. If you want to stay in your seats, then by all means do that.

"But whatever you do, do it because it's what you really feel inside."

Then I concluded by saying, "I'm going to see Ian someday . . . and I hope you will too."

When I walked off the stage, Bob came forward with a microphone. He cued Bryan to continue playing, and then, in a soft, dramatic voice, he asked the audience to stand.

Bob said, "It's just like Austin said: We're not here to scare anyone into accepting Christ tonight. We're not here to guilt anyone into coming forward. This is all about Jesus tonight."

He paused. "So, I want you to close your eyes."

He walked back and forth slowly. "Now, with your heads bowed and your eyes closed, I'd like you to raise your hand if you feel like you want to know Jesus Christ . . . if you feel like you've never asked him into your heart and you'd like to be saved tonight."

I wasn't surprised.

From my position backstage, I had a full view of the audience. There were no hands raised.

"Thank you," I watched Bob say to no one. "I see a couple of hands. Thank you."

Before he was done, Bob went through the entire formula, completely contradicting everything I had said. And because no one *really* lifted their hands, Bob began asking the all-inclusive questions: "Do any of you feel you're living with sin?" "Do any of you want to grow closer to God tonight?"

And of course, by the time Bob opened the altar, at least a hundred people came forward.

Which was fine.

I knew this would happen as soon as Bob told me the event *had* to have an invitation. I knew this was code for: "The youth leaders who brought their youth groups won't come back next year if none of their kids get saved."

I was familiar with this mentality, and I understood it well. I left the event that night feeling good about what I had said—hoping some of my words had been inspiring and praying that no one left feeling like a number.

The Jack Butler Way

KIDS: Dad, you're doing it wrong!
JACK BUTLER: Yeah, well, I'm doing it the Jack
Butler way.

—*Mr. Mom*, 1983

When I was twenty-one years old I dropped out of school. At the time it didn't really occur to me that leaving college without plans of enrolling in another officially made me a dropout. Looking back, I suppose I might have put more thought into leaving school if I'd known it would.

I mean, it's such an ugly term, *dropout*.

I associate it with this dude I knew in sixth grade, Mark Maddox. While the rest of us in sixth grade were eleven turning twelve, Mark was fifteen turning sixteen. He used to beat people up for fun, walk around the boys' locker room naked (because, well, let's face it: he was three years ahead of everyone else in his maturation), and brag about how he was soon getting his driver's license. Then somewhere between the end of sixth grade and the beginning of seventh, Mark disappeared. I was told later that he had "dropped out," a term I had heard mentioned before, but never related to someone I knew. It didn't take much sagacity to read between the lines and understand that when one spoke of Mark being a dropout, it was akin to saying he was a loser.

Honestly, we thought then, *who drops out of school?*

Turns out, I do.

In the spring of 2001, I packed my bags and left college in Lynchburg, Virginia, without a degree. Two months later I was living in an astronomically priced one-bedroom apartment in Atlanta, convinced that I was going to be a famous actor. Never mind that I had never acted before, that I had never taken an acting class, and that I didn't even *know* anyone who acted.

I was going to be the next big thing.

Well, two months into my tenure as an "actor" in Atlanta, not only had I not booked an acting gig, I had yet to even find a "side job."

You see, my original plan had been to land a gig as a bartender, figuring it would be good money, good times, and, most important, a good way to free up my days for auditioning. Therefore, just before leaving my hometown of High Point I signed up to get my bartending license.

Getting a bartending license seemed like the logical thing to do considering that I did, in fact, want to be a bartender. Turns out that bartending school is a brilliant scam, because one doesn't actually *need* a license to bartend. Furthermore, it turns out there actually is no such *thing* as a bartending license (even though I have one).

Once in Atlanta, I found out that bartending school is the mother of all jokes to working bartenders, especially in major cities, where bartenders aren't just young folks looking to make some money and have a good time, but are adults who consider bartending their occupation. For these professionals it is considered a rite of passage for novices to learn the bartending trade from older, more experienced bartenders. Circumventing this system by getting a "bartending degree" is like a kid cracking the starting lineup in Little League because his daddy bought the uniforms.

Still, my bartending license and I traveled all over greater Atlanta, hoping to find someone, anyone, willing to employ me. Two months later I had not received a single callback, let alone a job.

Meanwhile I bombed every acting audition I was sent on (it turns out I'm a bad actor). I was living in an apartment I couldn't afford, and my parents told me they were going to stop sending me money if I didn't get a job within the next month.

Let's just say things weren't going the way I had anticipated.

I had been unemployed in Atlanta for about two and a half months when I read about a new place opening up called the East Andrews Cafe and Bar. The ad in the newspaper said the management was actively hiring bartenders, and after a quick MapQuest search, I found that the bar was located only two miles from my apartment.

So far, so good.

I called and inquired about getting an interview, and three hours later I was already preparing for it. I stood in front of my mirror in a pair of khakis and a nice button-down shirt, looking presentable; just like the bartending school taught me. The man I spoke with on the phone said the management was currently sitting down with applicants and that I should come by in about four hours for an interview. After smoothing out my Dockers and adjusting my belt, I checked the clock. I still had about an hour before I had to be there.

So far so good.

When I got to the bar, there was a lot of renovation being done to the building, both inside and out. I was about fifteen minutes early (as the bartending school advised), and upon arriving I took a seat in the courtyard with about five other guys who were also applying to be bartenders. All of these guys were about seven to ten years older than me, and they were all wearing jeans and T-shirts, laughing with one another as if they were all in on the same joke. I was left to assume that my pressed oxford was the punch line.

Finally, after about an hour of waiting, I was ushered to the rear of the building to have an interview with the head bartender, Steve. After walking through a maze of two-by-fours, sawdust, and electrical power tools, I found a man with a bright smile and puffy red cheeks waiting at a high table. Walking up to him, I said, "Are you Steve?"

"Steve de Haan," he said, extending a palm toward me.

I sat with Steve for about thirty minutes, more than long enough to find out that he had placed sixth in the world for "flair bartending," and long enough to find out that flair bartending meant flipping bottles the way Tom Cruise did in *Cocktail*. In those thirty minutes, I also learned that all but one of the bartenders East Andrews would employ were world-recognized flair bartenders and that the one who wasn't, a man named Brendan, had been a staple in the Atlanta nightlife for the past fifteen years. Steve told me that the bar was looking to hire just one more bartender, and that they had over twenty-five applicants hoping to fill that slot.

"So what makes you think you should be the one?"

Steve asked me, sitting back and folding his hands in his lap.

"Umm . . . I have a bartending degree," I replied.

Steve cackled. "You fell in that trap, huh?"

I nodded.

"Well," he said, "usually that is the kiss of death around here." He paused. "But I sense something special about you."

I wondered if it was the Polo Sport I had squirted on my shirt collar. "I'm a hard worker," I said quickly. (This was a lie: I'm not a hard worker.)

"Everyone applying is a hard worker," Steve said.

"I'm a quick study too." (This was also a lie: I am probably the slowest study in the whole world.)

Steve scratched his chin. "Well," he finally said, "the truth is, we are actually looking for someone young and inexperienced. We want to find someone we can train to be the Brian Flanagan of Atlanta."

"Brian Flanagan?"

"That was Tom Cruise's name in *Cocktail*."

"Oh, yeah. Gotcha. Good flick."

"We want to train this person to be a flair bartender and eventually put him behind the main bar."

I nodded.

"Do you think you could do this?"

I began picturing myself as Brian Flanagan, effort-lessly tossing bottles in the air, entertaining the entire bar with my charm before going home to make out with Gina Gershon and/or Elisabeth Shue.

"I think I can manage it," I replied.

Steve ran a hand through his hair and sat forward. "Now, the catch is, you'll have to start as a barback. Are you okay with that?"

I didn't have the slightest clue what a "barback" was. To be honest, I'd never even heard the term before.

"Of course," I replied, nodding adamantly. "I planned to start as a barback anyway."

Steve grinned. He stuck his arm across the table. "Congratulations," he said. "The job is yours."

He excused himself a minute later, and I was left to navigate my way through the construction on my own. When I made it back to my car, it dawned on me what had just happened: I had finally landed a real job. I had found my temporary calling.

So far, so good.

The first month of my employment at East Andrews Cafe consisted of the following:

1. *Numerous all-staff training events. Translation: learning every nuance of the menu while learning absolutely nothing about being a barback.*
2. *Five mandatory wine tastings, wherein the staff*

was responsible for helping select the wines the restaurant would feature. Translation: the staff getting sloppy drunk and shamelessly flirting with one another.

3. *Manual labor to help finalize the renovations. Translation: sleeping off my hangovers from the mandatory wine tastings under the staircase I was supposed to be painting.*

Finally, after a month of training, the bar was set to have its grand opening, which promised to be a huge deal, seeing as East Andrews had received favorable write-ups in many publications throughout the Atlanta area.

For my part, I was totally prepared to be East Andrews's barback, except for one minor detail: I still didn't know what a barback *was*.

I got to the bar at 4:45 p.m. opening day, uniform on, just as I had been instructed. As soon as I got to the building, I clocked in and went looking for Brendan, who had emerged as my mentor. I found him behind the main bar, working to fill one of the garnish trays.

"What's up, dawg?" he said, looking up at me over a jar of olives.

"Chillin', bro," I said, trying not to let my nervousness show. "What you need me to do?"

Brendan scratched his Mr. Clean head. "We need some more lemons. Have you ever sliced lemons?"

"Of course," I nodded, even though I'd never sliced a lemon in my life.

"Great," Brendan said. "There are several boxes in the back. Go ahead and knock out a full box."

"I'm on it."

I walked back into the kitchen where several people were busy at work. I inquired as to the whereabouts of the lemon boxes, and one of the cooks grunted toward the far corner. I saw a box with several drawings of big yellow lemons on the side and went to grab it. Picking it up, it weighed far more than I had imagined. After looking inside, I realized why: there were roughly seventeen billion lemons inside.

I shook my head, thinking it would take me an eternity to cut them all. Then I looked around the kitchen, realizing that now that I had the lemons, I needed to learn how to slice them. I was hoping to be able to do this without having to ask anyone, because I am the type of person who hates to admit that I don't know how to do something.

After taking a quick inventory of the kitchen, I noted that one of the cooks was using a cutting board to chop some parsley.

Therefore I went and grabbed a knife and a cutting board.

Then, after putting the cutting board beside my box, I grabbed my first lemon. I glanced around to see if anyone was watching and, realizing no one was paying attention, I steadied the lemon with my left hand while pressing the knife against it with my right.

I didn't even get the lemon half cut.

You see, because of the bogus way I was holding my lemon, it slipped right out from under the knife and left my pointer finger lying limp against the cutting board. As the knife came down, blood erupted from my finger immediately, in a red geyser that drew the attention of everyone in the kitchen. Within five minutes Brendan had rushed back to assess the cut. After staring at my finger like he was a doctor (and staring at me like I was an idiot), he alerted the general manager/owner that I had sliced my finger and would require several stitches.

So ten minutes later, on the night his bar was having its grand opening, the owner found himself driving me to the hospital on Peachtree, where he waited with me for two hours before a doctor got around to stitching me up.

In summation: the bar was officially open for thirty minutes before I got sidelined due to injury.

So much for "so far, so good."

One week, a bottle of Vicodin, a truckload of Tylenol, a case of Miller Lite, and four missed shifts later, my finger wound and I were ready to get back to work. In the week that I was away, East Andrews had become a hit. The bar had filled to capacity every night and word was spreading through Atlanta that it was the new hot spot. When I heard these reports from my apartment, they made me anxious to return to barbacking. Even if I *had* only barbacked for thirty minutes in my illustrious career, and even if I *didn't* technically know what a barback was . . . still, I had the distinct feeling that the bar needed me.

It was a Thursday night when I returned, and, upon parting the French doors and stepping into the room, I entered a hero, a man proven: a man who'd been bloodied in battle. Even if the entire staff thought I was an idiot, even if my finger was wrapped like an Egyptian mummy, still mine was a much-heralded return, an occurrence that broke up the monotony of everyone's daily bar preparations. I greeted my coworkers with big smiles and much self-deprecation. I lingered around the girls from the wait-staff who felt it necessary to mother me with their concern. "Oh, it's fine," I told them over and over. "It was just a small cut. I'm such an idiot. Really, it's fine. I mean, I've had worse injuries from playing college soccer. Have I ever mentioned to you that I played college soccer?"

When the fanfare died down, I clocked in and went to find Brendan.

This time he was in the liquor closet, stocking up on bottles of Grand Marnier.

"What's up, man?" I said, my voice cracking as I tried to stand confidently before him.

Brendan, who was bent over, twisted to look at me. The top of his bald head was shining as it caught the reflection of the overhead light. "Austin—hey, big guy. How's the finger?"

"Healing up just right," I said. "What can I do for you?"

Brendan pried two more bottles loose and then stood up straight. He studied me. "I'm almost afraid to say."

"Lemons?" I asked.

Brendan nodded.

"I'm on it," I said, wheeling to head back to the massive lemon box from which I'd cut precisely zero lemons the week before.

"The hell you are," he said, walking past me with his hands full of Grand Marnier bottles. He motioned with his head to a couple of stray bottles sitting loose on the shelf. "Grab those other two Grand Ma bottles and follow me to the bar. We'll stock these, and then I'm going to show you the *right* way to slice a lemon. You know, the way that doesn't cost you a finger."

"Cool," I said, grabbing the two liquor bottles. I followed behind him. "Why are you getting out so much Grand Marnier?" I asked.

"It was Service Industry Night last night," he said.

"And in this town the service industry folks shoot Grand Ma like it's water."

"Gotcha," I said, even though I didn't.

We put the bottles away, and then I followed him into the kitchen. Brendan grabbed a cutting board and then found a knife that looked very different from the one I'd used the week before.

"You see this knife?" he asked. "See this blade? The way it has ridges? This is called a serrated knife." He was speaking slowly to me, as if I were a pet or a child.

"Can you repeat that?" he said. "*Suh-ray-tid*."

"*Suh-ray-tid*."

Brendan nodded. "That's right, serrated. It is less dangerous than that Rambo knife you bludgeoned your finger with last week."

"Don't worry, man," I said, desperately trying to win his confidence again. "I know I messed up, but it won't happen again."

"I know. I believe you," Brendan said. Then he clapped his hands and took a deep breath. "Now," he said, reaching under the table and grabbing the huge box of lemons, "let's show you how to cut these things the right way."

After a five-minute demonstration on how to properly slice a lemon, along with repeated promises that I wouldn't cut off another part of my finger, Brendan left me alone to slice the entire box of lemons.

About thirty minutes later, I had succeeded.

Now, I've never been so proud of myself for having completed something so elementary in my entire life. You would have thought I had just climbed Mount Everest the way I walked up to Brendan where he stood behind the main bar, my tub of freshly sliced lemons cradled against my chest.

Brendan looked up and, seeing what was in my hands, began clapping. Then, as the other two bartenders turned their attention to me, they too began clapping. The gathered applause drew the gazes of several members of the waitstaff, who, seeing my full tub, also began clapping. The next thing I knew, the entire room was applauding my triumphant feat.

With my face glowing crimson, I bowed like a conductor at Carnegie Hall.

Several hours later the bar was slammed. My accomplishment with the lemons had been long forgotten, as the bar lines were snaking six people deep, everyone clamoring for the bartenders' attention.

In the two hours following my lemon cutting, I had quickly figured out what a barback *really* was: the bartender's stooge. The barback, I learned, was really just a glorified busboy, an errand runner responsible for restocking the bartender's cooler, restocking the bartender's liquor wells, restocking the bartender's ice, taking out the bartender's trash, combing the bartender's hair, feeding the bartender, and making sure the bartender's shoes were always tied.

In other words, being a barback *sucked*.

Anyway, I had been running around frantically the whole evening, trying my best to cement my status as "worst barback in Atlanta history," when Brendan asked me about apple slices.

Now, at this point I must confess: I could not *possibly* have been more inept at barbacking. When Brendan asked for a bottle of vodka, I invariably showed up with a bottle of gin. When Brendan asked for more lemons, I showed up with more limes. I didn't know the difference between Captain Morgan and Captain Hook, let alone the contents of a harvey wallbanger or a screaming orgasm. Bartending school had been a *huge* waste of time. Meanwhile, because of my major case of ADD, I spent most of my time spacing out behind the bar, gazing distantly at the walls, completely oblivious to the bartenders screaming my name.

At around midnight, Brendan turned to me in a frenzy. He yelled my name, snapping me out of one of my daydreams.

"Austin?" He clapped his hands. *"Austin!"*

Coming to, I turned to him.

His eyes were black marbles. "We need apple slices

for the Washington-apple martinis—and we need them on the fly," he said.

"On the *fly*?" I asked.

Brendan looked around, as if completely exasperated. "*Now*, you putz," he screamed. "It means we need them *now*!"

"Gotcha," I said. I turned to rush to the kitchen but then realized I didn't have the slightest clue where the apple slices were kept.

"Where are they?" I said, turning back, scared to ask the question.

"That's what I'm trying to tell you. We don't *have* anymore. We totally underestimated how many we'd need. We need you to go slice some more."

"I'm on it!" I said. I turned to run to the back.

"Austin?" Brendan said, stopping me cold.

I wheeled around.

"Have you ever used an apple slicer?"

Everything in me wanted to say yes; I felt the word bubbling at my lips. However, I remembered what a fiasco this same lie created just a week before and I sheepishly ducked my head. "No."

Brendan sighed. "Here, quick, follow me," he said, scooting under the side of the bar and then sprinting to the kitchen.

I followed him to the back, where he unearthed some

contraption that looked very much like a cheese grater (which, I might add, I've never used either). Steadying the contraption, Brendan grabbed an apple and, with expert dexterity, began running it over the blades, leaving small apple slices in his wake.

"Do you see what I'm doing?" he asked.

I nodded.

"It's very simple."

I nodded again.

"All you have to do is make sure you keep your thumbs up, or else you'll take off part of your thumb."

I nodded again.

"Okay," he said, handing me the half of the apple he had yet to slice. "We need these on the fly."

"Gotcha. We need them *now*," I said, trying to demonstrate how strong my retention skills were.

Brendan shook his head, as if amazed at what a moron I was, and then sprinted back to the bar. Meanwhile I steadied myself over the apple slicer. Then I glanced at the half of the apple remaining and the slices Brendan had left beside it.

Simple, I whispered to myself.

I scratched my head and then buried myself in my work. And, because we needed these slices *on the fly*, I moved at a rapid pace. The bar needs me, I thought to myself, and I will deliver.

I made one successful slice, and then two, and then three. And then . . .

The blood squirted from my thumb like fruit punch from a water gun. I looked down at the wound, unable to see how deeply I'd cut myself because there was so much blood rushing forth. I was in pain, growing dizzy and light-headed, but my shame and embarrassment superseded my agony. I found a bar towel and wrapped it around my thumb. Then I rushed to the back of the kitchen, hoping, inexplicably, that I could somehow hide the wound from the entire staff.

Well, it turns out that hiding a partially severed thumb is kind of difficult.

I didn't make it thirty seconds before I was outed. In my flight to the back, one of the Latino dishwashers saw the red liquid spreading like a disease through the bar towel. He looked at me with incredulous eyes. "Oh no, amigo," he said. "No a-*geen*?!"

I ducked my head.

He shook his head, muttering "*Ay Dios mío*" as he went searching for someone to address my latest blunder.

Five minutes later Brendan was standing over me, peeling the bar towel back to get a clean look at the wound. Then, glancing up at me, his face devoid of all expression, he said, "You're missing a small chunk of your thumb." He paused. "You're going to have to go back to the hospital."

Ten minutes later I was sitting in the owner's car again, riding with him to the same hospital on Peachtree, sitting in the same waiting room I'd sat in a week earlier, and eventually being treated by the same nurse and the same doctor.

I guess it was around the time the owner dropped me off at my apartment, as I stood on the curb and watched his taillights disappear into the night, that I began thinking that maybe I wasn't cut out for the service industry after all.

The partially severed thumb kept me away from work for another two and a half weeks. To East Andrews Cafe's unbelievable credit, they didn't fire me. Even though I was, quite obviously, the most worthless employee on staff, the owners, after two trips to the hospital in one week, still seemed to like me. I think they viewed me with a mixture of pity and obligation, keeping me on simply because they believed me to be a genuine, sweet kid. I'm left to believe this because every time they'd reprimand me for doing something inane (which was roughly every other hour), they'd begin with: "Now, Austin, you're such a sweet and genuine kid, but . . ."

I ended up staying at East Andrews for about eight more months, and in that time I somehow managed to avoid a third trip to the hospital. But the reason I mention my wounds in Atlanta is because of what grew from the forced downtime they yielded. During those shiftless weeks, when I could not work, as I sat alone in my one-bedroom apartment, cursing myself for being a fool and pining for anything that might alleviate my boredom, I began writing my first novel.

The novel was a project I'd been thinking about for over a year but had never actually sat down and begun. But sitting in Atlanta, feeling down on my luck and watching the four walls of my apartment close in around me, I suddenly felt like it was now or never. That probably sounds a bit melodramatic, but it's how I felt. I started telling myself that I would likely never have this kind of downtime again.

With a story idea in my head and what looked like a mini beehive wrapped around my thumb, I sat down at my computer and began typing. (Now, in case you're wondering how I typed without the use of my thumb and with only partial use of my left pointer finger, let me explain: I have never taken a typing class. To this very day I type with a modified version of the hunt-and-peck method, and it works just fine for me.)

As the days passed and my manuscript got longer, I began realizing something about myself: I *loved* writing. That is to say, I had a passion for it, a passion unlike I'd ever felt for anything else. Sure I *liked* the idea of acting, but I didn't have the necessary drive for it. I didn't have the constitution it requires to be a real actor. I didn't have it in me to study the craft for hours a day, to part with my hard-earned money in order to pay for acting classes, to constantly get rejected at audition after audition.

But when it came to writing, something told me that no matter what, no matter how long it took, I was going to make it. No matter how many rejection letters, no matter how many failed manuscripts, no matter how many reassurances that it was impossible—I just *believed*. I felt something stirring inside me that I had never felt before. Later I'd realize it was *drive*.

As the manuscript neared completion, I began considering how I could best make writing a career. I knew the odds were against me, but I was willing to take the plunge. Consequently, I started confiding in people close to me, telling them that I was going to forgo acting and move back up to North Carolina, where I could live cheaply and focus on writing. Invariably, every one of the people I confided in told me to grow up, to get back in school and focus on getting my degree.

Everyone, that is, except my dad.

I told my old man how everyone I knew was telling me I was foolish, that I was wasting my potential, and that I needed to get a degree and get a real job. Very calmly, he said something I'll never forget:

"Austin, *everyone* wants to tell everyone else how to live their own life."

Then my dad—who everyone calls Seadog—encouraged me to continue walking the path less traveled. He pointed out how most of the people who were telling me to get back in school and find a real job seemed unhappy with their own lives. Seadog explained that I was in a position in which I would never find myself again: I was young and unattached; I had only myself to answer to. Seadog said that most people his age, after doing things the way society told them they were supposed to, often found themselves looking back on being young and unencumbered and wishing they had taken more chances. Seadog told me that getting a job and a degree just because I felt *obligated* to get a job and a degree was the same thing as putting myself in prison. He said that I should never do something simply because I felt I was *supposed* to do it, but rather, while I still could, to do things because I *wanted* to do them. "You won't always have that opportunity," he said. "One day you'll be responsible for a wife, for a family, and once that happens, you won't have the luxury of being able to do what you want to do, because you'll have more people to think about than just yourself."

Then he said: "There is no right way to make a life for yourself. These things aren't black and white. There's no set way to live your life. Take a look around. How many people actually seem happy?"

"Very few," I muttered.

"Exactly," he said. "The name of the game is living with as few regrets as possible, and most people are living with a whole world of regrets. So don't worry about people telling you you're doing it wrong. Just let that go in one ear and out the other."

"That's easier said than done," I said.

Seadog laughed and then cited one of our favorite movies, *Mr. Mom.* "Well, no one said it'd be easy doing it the Jack Butler way."

To conclude, I'll spare you the details of my last six years trying to become a published writer. Suffice it to say that those six years were full of seemingly endless rejections and lots of heartache. In my quest for publication, I have written over one million unpublished words, and I have been rejected by over a hundred literary agencies (and by over fifty publishing houses). However, I would not trade the rejections or the heartache for anything, because they have taught me something infinitely valuable.

If we really want something, if we really believe in it, it *is* possible to grab it. And while this may be the most tired cliché, it is the most important one to repeat, because the pervasive mentality of today's culture runs counter to its message.

The majority of the time, seeking out the things we most want requires making unconventional and sometimes unpopular decisions. This can be scary, which is what stops so many of us in our tracks before we've even taken the first step. It's why so many of us talk about daring to be different, but so few of us actually try.

I find it very telling that so many in my generation cite Paulo Coelho's *The Alchemist* as one of our favorite books; yet so few of us allow ourselves to follow the story's message: to listen to our hearts and follow our dreams.

It is true that we all have different sacrifices we need to make in order to pursue what we really love. And it's true that some of us have tougher roads than others. But the point is not about the difficulty of the journey; it is about the power of perseverance and the spiritual reward we receive through doing what we have to do in order to keep our dreams alive.

The book you are reading, and the fulfillment that writing it has given me, are a testament to this truth.

As I reflect on all of the failed acting auditions, on all of the cuts and wounds from barbacking, on all of the patience and kindness from mentors like Brendan, and on all of the rejections and heartbreak, I now know that Seadog was absolutely right: that there is no set formula for happiness. Even if it does cost us some time or some pride or some sacrifice, or even if it costs us a piece of our thumb, as long as we keep doing things the Jack Butler way, we can never go wrong.

Chicks Dig Ace

Being the third most famous reality television star in my postal code is not a job I take lightly. In fact all three of us who represent High Point, North Carolina, take our positions very seriously. And although our responsibilities vary in nature, they are all equally important. We all work very hard to manage our respective task loads. The fact that the two more famous stars in our coalition have never, in fact, met me does not hurt our ability to work together. Nor does the fact that the other two don't know that we're working together. Moreover, it hasn't even seemed to matter that the other two don't even know I exist.

As a team, we're just that good.

Our record suggests that, together, the three of us are making our community very proud. Lately though, it has come to our (my) attention that some people are unclear as to the organization of our hierarchy and what

I actually contribute to the cause. Since I believe that this information should be a matter of public record, I have listed our pecking order and job descriptions below.

(Un)official Bureau of High Point Reality Stars

Chris Daughtry (President)

Chris sells millions of albums, tours with Bon Jovi, and consistently appears on television shows like *Ellen*, *The Tonight Show*, and *Late Night*.

Fantasia Barrino (Vice President)

Fantasia sells tons of records, headlines in plays on Broadway, appears on shows like *Oprah* and *The View*, and has a sign in her honor, just off the highway, that proclaims High Point the "Home of Fantasia Barrino."

Austin Carty (Intern)

Austin eats at places like High Point's Burger King and Pizza Hut, where, every once in a while, people approach him and say, "Hey, weren't you on television? On that show *Survivor*, right? Yeah, that *was* you! Man, that's crazy!" Then they pause for a moment before adding, "Now, what was your name again?"

• • •

So, as you can clearly see, each member of our triumvirate has a very important role to play. In some ways we are very much like a democratic body, a coalition modeled after the U.S. government. We have three separate but equal branches; each of us understands that true democracy rests in a strong system of checks and balances (Chris and Fantasia collect check after check while I balance a negative bank account).

Now, some people wonder whether I ever get the tiniest bit frustrated that my role is slightly "less glamorous" than Chris's or Fantasia's.

The answer is no.

Of course I don't.

You see, I am our voice on the ground. I am our Dan Rather. Our Katie Couric. Our Geraldo-at-large. What people fail to understand is that, while Chris and Fantasia jet-set around the world, performing concerts to sold-out crowds and doing important work with international charities, I am the one who stays behind in our hometown, ready to face our constituents, ready to field the important questions about what it was like being on reality television. Whether people realize it or not, answering these questions is a very important part of our job. And I am happy to serve as the team's local voice. So while Chris and Fantasia handle interviews with folks like Jay Leno and Dave Letterman, I stay behind and give interviews like this one to strangers at the local 7-Eleven:

Hey, man . . . Is Survivor *real?*
Yes.
Like, they don't give you any help?
No.
You mean to tell me that the producers don't give you any food at all?
Not a morsel.
Well, then what did you eat while you were out there?
Ants, hermit crabs, snails . . . termites.
Really?
Really.
Would you ever do it again?
Yeah, I would.
Really?
Really.
So how'd you get on the show?
Well, by accident, really. My sister used to be Miss Teen North Carolina several years ago, and because of her pageant affiliation, I got asked to judge a few pageants. I was judging Miss Pennsylvania one year, and one of the judges happened to work in casting for CBS. She told me I should apply.
So, what is Jeff Probst like?

He's great; he's a very likable guy whose smarts are overlooked because he is the host of a reality television program.

Yeah, I like him . . . So, what was the most memorable part of your time on Survivor?

That's easy: I got to be friends with an astronaut. He's this amazing, brilliant, humble man named Dan Barry, who didn't tell me until the twelfth day that he was an astronaut—that he had been in space three times. To be honest with you, that's the most memorable thing that's *ever* happened to me. How many people can say they've sat down with a friend who has been in space and discussed what it's like to look at Earth from orbit? I count myself really lucky to have had an opportunity like that.

Cool . . . So, what happens to you when you get voted out?

Well it varies from location to location. During my season, we got sent to this awesome little villa that was on its own island. I recall someone telling me that Michael Bolton used to own it, but that could have been a lie.

So did you just start eating right away?

Absolutely. Like a wild animal. As soon as you get to the villa, you give the contestant manager your wish list: you know, all the foods and drinks you'd like to have. Then they do what they can to get them.

Do you really see lots of snakes out there?

Yeah.

Have you ever met Richard Hatch?

No.

How about that guy with the beard? What's his name? Rupert?

Yeah, Rupert. Have you met him?

Yes. He's a nice guy.

So, what's it like being famous?

I don't know. I'm not famous.

But people know your name when you go places, right?

I guess here in High Point they do sometimes. But it doesn't happen nearly as much as when my show was actually on TV.

Well, what's it like when it does happen?

It's often very flattering. A false ego boost, if you will. But to be honest, it can sometimes be humiliating.

Humiliating?

Yeah.

How?

Well, it was only really humiliating this one time. It was about two weeks into the airing of my season of *Survivor*. I was in Charlotte with a couple of friends, and we had gone to some bar with a weird name, something like Jackalopes. We hadn't been there for twenty minutes before word started spreading through the place that someone from *Survivor* was in the bar.

This was very new for me at this point, and I was

caught off guard by how many people were suddenly turkey-necking for a better look at me. I mean, I'm sure that none of them actually *cared* that I was on *Survivor*. It's just that, down where we come from, people from television aren't always hanging around the bars, you know?

Well, suddenly, out of nowhere, this drunken redneck dude came rushing up to me and stopped just short of my nose. He stuck his finger in my face and said, "Man, you look just like that dude from TV!"

He seemed kind of angry, so I was a little nervous. I said, "I . . . I do?"

And he just kind of nodded. But then, suddenly, he smiled. And because he smiled, I relaxed, figuring he must be a *Survivor* fan. So I puffed my chest out, all full of ego, and said, "So I look like someone from TV, huh? Who do you think I look like?"

I was waiting for him to say, "Austin from *Survivor*," of course, but the guy looked me right in the eye and said, "Man, you look just like Ace from *American Idol*!"

Talk about deflating someone's balloon. I said, "I . . . I do?"

And the drunk dude, not missing a beat, said, "Oh yeah, man, totally. But I hope that don't offend you or nothing. Cause chicks dig Ace!"

"Chicks dig Ace?" I repeated.

The guy nodded. "Oh heck yeah, man! Chicks are

crazy about Ace!" He smacked me on the shoulder and then walked away.

Ten minutes later I had forgotten all about the guy, but then I saw him talking excitedly to someone on the other side of the bar. Apparently he was still hung up on the idea that I looked like Ace from *American Idol*. What he didn't realize was that the guy he was talking to was one of the people I'd come to the bar with. The next thing I knew, I saw my buddy pointing at me, his expression curious.

Turns out the drunk dude had pulled my buddy aside and said, "Man, you see that guy over there? He looks just like Ace from *American Idol*."

My friend pointed to me and said, "Him?"

And the drunk dude nodded.

My buddy said, "Well, I suppose he *kind of* looks like him. But he looks *a lot* like Austin from *Survivor*."

The drunk dude squinted in my direction for a better look. Then, turning back to my friend, he said, "I guess he *kind of* looks like him. But he looks *way* more like Ace from *American Idol*."

So there you have it. Sometimes when I go places, lots of people know my name. Other times, people think I'm Ace from *American Idol*.

Man, that's some story.

Thanks.

Well, I have to be running now, but it was great meet-ing you. Our family loved you on the show.

Thank you. I really appreciate you saying that.

Anytime. You take care now. Wait, I'm sorry, what was your name again?

Austin.

Yeah, sorry about that. You take care, Austin.

So as you can see, I have serious responsibilities to uphold. I know that Fantasia and Chris wish they could be here with me, working for the community at the grassroots level, but the simple truth is that we can't all be in one place at one time. So while they continue to travel the globe, I stay behind—taking one for the team, so to speak—and make sure that the local residents are well informed on subjects like how hermit crabs taste and what being at a tribal council is like.

It's a tough job, but for the sake of the coalition, I carry on.

Now, I'm obviously kidding. Though we do live in the same small town, Fantasia Barrino and Chris Daughtry have no idea who I am. Moreover, they are real celebrities who contribute worthwhile entertainment to the world. I'm just a guy who once ate some termites and snails.

Luckily for me though, I never totally confused my quick stint on reality television with true celebrity. I realized quickly that just because I spent a couple of weeks starving on an island didn't mean I should be moving to LA and starving beside Mary-Kate and Ashley at Geisha House.

However, while it might seem fairly obvious that spending a couple of weeks trying to win the love of Bret Michaels or Flava Flav doesn't make you a bona fide star, somehow, against logic, many of us who've been on reality television confuse our five seconds of fame with legitimate celebrity. Consequently, Los Angeles is teeming with one-time reality stars trying to become actors. However, when my season of *Survivor* ended, I opted to settle back into my normal life in High Point, where I remain today.

Having said that, I confess there *was* a time, just after *Survivor* ended, when I considered moving to LA or New York. A couple of soap operas had expressed interest in me (well, vague interest), and I found myself magnetically drawn to the idea of larger celebrity even though I had already traveled down the acting road once and found that it wasn't for me. Luckily, just as I was contemplating this big move, I got asked to speak at a high school in Florida.

Initially, I was a bit anxious because I was going to be addressing a group of people who were just a few years younger than I was. I knew the school's administrators were expecting me to deliver profound words of wisdom, a message that would help the students enter society as better people. But how was I supposed to do that?

I mean, what do I know?

I remember hunching over my computer late into the night as I struggled to get down my thoughts, the cursor blinking back at me from an empty screen. I wanted to write a deep, poetic address about how I had learned to be a responsible adult and how, if the students would just follow my advice, they too could become happy, responsible adults.

But then it occurred to me: I *wasn't* a responsible adult. Most days I slept in until ten. I didn't have a real job or even a college degree. I had about a hundred dollars in the bank, and the only food I knew how to cook was a peanut butter and jelly sandwich. The only reason I was addressing these students was that I'd been on reality television. How did that make me an expert on growing up?

Realizing I would be seen as a fraud if I went the "responsible" route, I decided to take a new approach. I cranked up the radio and began typing furiously, not trying to produce a flowery, encouraging piece of oratory, but rather simple thoughts based on my own experiences. I worked into the wee hours of the morning, and just as I was shutting down my computer a song by the band Switchfoot came on the radio. Though I had heard it many times, this was the first time I had truly digested its lyrics.

The song offered a haunting message, one that stopped me cold that night. As the final bars hummed through the radio speakers, I found myself surveying the state of my life, thinking about the decisions I was facing concerning my future. The next thing I knew, I had ruled out moving to New York or LA, and I jumped back into my computer chair, reopened my speech, and added the song's lyrics, believing it imperative that the message I'd discovered make it into my address.

Two days later I was in Florida, sitting onstage at the high school. In my pocket was a copy of my speech. Although it had not turned out emotional or poetic, I felt it carried a message to which young adults could relate.

When the school's principal called my name, I strode to the podium. Looking over the crowd of teenagers, I told them how fascinated I have always been by art—by books, paintings, and music. I told the students how I find it amazing that a few strokes of a brush, or a few words strung together in the right order, or certain lyrics set against just the right melody, can change someone's life forever.

Then I told them how art had just changed my life—how, with eleven simple words, a band called Switchfoot had recently inspired me to make a major decision about my future.

After a long pause, I told them what those eleven words were:

This is your life. Are you who you want to be?

This might sound like a simple question, but to me it is a painfully *deep* question and if correctly applied to one's life it can be penetrating to the core.

To me these lyrics are telling us to take inventory of our lives. To really think about our plans for the future.

They are asking us to think about what type of college we want to attend. What kind of career we want to have. What kind of person we want to marry. What kind of wife or husband or parent we want to be. How we want others to perceive us. How we want to be remembered.

Then, once we have a picture of our chosen future crystallized in our head, I think they are asking us to throw it away. To pretend like it doesn't exist.

Next—not overtly, but I think it's in there—they tell us to do the converse: to picture everything we have done in our past—the good and the bad.

They tell us that even if we're the person who constantly gives money to our church, who constantly bakes pies for our neighbors, who has forgiven our partner for cheating on us, who slaves every day in a job we hate just to support a family who doesn't appreciate us . . .

Or even if we are the person who has cheated on our spouse. Even if we're an alcoholic. A drug addict. A sex addict. A thief. A liar . . .

These lyrics are telling us to throw our pasts away, to pretend like they don't exist.

Then they are saying to look at what we have after we've thrown out the past and the future.

Now do you see it?

This little strand of days.

Today and tomorrow.

Right now.

This is your life. Not all of that other stuff. Don't be fooled. *This*, today.

This is your life.

Are you who you want to be?

After I explained all that to the students, I went on to tell them about my experiences growing up.

You see, I had a whole plan mapped out for my future, even though I didn't consciously *know* I did. I had planned on being a college graduate with a wife and a couple of children, on being some sort of salesman and owning a house with a nice backyard. I figured I would be the model father and the model husband, and, to round it all out, I would be the model Christian.

Like I said, I never sat down and *planned* any of this. This picture had just, through the years, taken shape inside my head. I think this happens to all of us. I think we rarely realize when we are doing our deepest contemplation regarding our own lives, because it takes place subconsciously.

Looking back, I think I was under a false impression that there are two stages of life, adolescence and adulthood, and that between them there is a bridge linking one to the other. I figured that when I finally crossed the bridge and stepped into adulthood, I would know it and I would make the switch. I would grow up and be mature and responsible. Just like that. I assumed it was at this juncture that I would start acting like the committed Christian I wanted to be and, soon thereafter, a perfect woman would enter my life and she and I would marry and start producing little wunderkinder.

But here's what I found out: there is no bridge.

I've found that the decisions we make today affect the person we will be tomorrow (and I don't mean that metaphorically, I mean literally *tomorrow*), and before we know it, tomorrow turns into the next day and then into the next.

And then a week passes.

And then a month.

And then a year.

And then another year.

And then maybe five years.

Or maybe ten years.

Or, who knows, maybe even *forty* years.

But at some point, for some unforeseen reason, life finally gets hold of us and we find ourselves looking in the mirror (now I *am* speaking metaphorically) and asking: How did I get here? This isn't where I planned on being at this point. This isn't what I planned on doing with my life. How did I get *here*?

And the answer is very simple. It is one I have learned through experience: we start snowballing.

We make one small mistake one day, opening ourselves up to make the same small mistake the next day. Then these small mistakes lead to making other, slightly bigger, mistakes. And then, eventually, we no longer consider these mistakes to be mistakes because, suddenly, they no longer *are* mistakes.

They are our lives.

I went on to explain to the students how, until I heard that song by Switchfoot, I had been snowballing. I had been considering moving to Los Angeles to try to become an actor, even though I had tried it once before and knew that being an actor wasn't what I really wanted. I had allowed my slight brush with reality television fame to convince me that I really did deserve to be famous. I had bathed in the praise and affirmation of strangers, and consequently I had become drawn to Los Angeles to seek more of it.

But hearing those words had caused me to realize that

I wanted to go to Los Angeles for the wrong reasons, that I didn't want to be an actor because I respected it as an art form, but because I just wanted people to see me on TV. I had become like all those other reality television has-beens that I had always made fun of.

And as I wrapped up my speech, I told the students that, because of the Switchfoot song, I had decided to stay where I felt I belonged, to keep plugging away at what I really loved and felt passionate about (writing), even if it never did yield true "success" or bring me any real recognition. I told them that I, thankfully, had realized I didn't need to pursue fame in order to be content with my life. I could leave fame to other people—people truly talented and suited for it, like Chris Daughtry and Fantasia Barrino.

Then, in closing, I told the students that *this* was their life.

Not yesterday.

Not tomorrow.

Today.

Then I asked them a simple question: are you who you want to be?

The students kindly clapped for me as I took a seat, and a couple hours later, when I got to the airport, I began reflecting on the speech, thinking about how thankful I was that I had heard that Switchfoot song and how thankful I was to be heading back to High Point where I belonged. Because in so doing I was being who I wanted to be.

I was being Ace from *American Idol*.

And from what I had been told, chicks dig Ace.

Amway-ing for Jesus

During the summer following my freshman year of college, my buddy Kevin invited me to go on a beach trip with his family. On the first night, he and I went walking along the beach, hoping to pick up girls (which was, of course, our purpose for going on the trip in the first place). We soon stumbled upon a hippie dude sitting alone on a boardwalk, picking his guitar. He looked to be in his midtwenties, and, in the glow of the moonlight, the shiny streaks on his cheeks suggested he'd been crying. Upon seeing us, the hippie composed himself and offered us a seat. Then, motioning to a case of Busch Light, he asked if we wanted a beer. For two eighteen-year-olds without fake IDs this was like hitting the lottery. We quickly cracked open two cans before he could change his mind.

My memories of the hippie are hazy now, so I don't recall his name, but I'm pretty sure he told it to us. He had curly brown hair that fell just below his chin, and each angle of his face was sharp and pronounced. Because this is all I'm able to remember, I recall him looking just like Gavin Rossdale of the band Bush (pre–Gwen Stefani). He had a gaunt figure, and though I have no basis for this, when I think of him now I picture him wearing a Phish T-shirt (seeing as this was the standard uniform for most wannabe hippies in the late nineties).

The hippie told us that he had a girlfriend with whom he had conceived a baby girl. This girlfriend had recently left him in the middle of the night, taking the baby with her. He must have played "Let Her Cry" by Hootie and the Blowfish at least twenty times in the hour that Kevin and I sat with him, and I remember not being able to understand why he liked that song so much.

I am nothing if not slow on the uptake.

This was the summer before I learned to play guitar, something I'd been vowing to do since middle school. Since I didn't realize that most of the songs he was playing were, from a technical perspective, rather rudimentary, I thought I had stumbled on Bob Dylan. I asked him to play almost every song I could think of, and he obliged by playing the ones he knew. I thought the hippie was intriguing, living out of his car and playing guitar for no one but the seagulls and the ocean. He used words like *nah* and *man* in every sentence and kept a wad of Skoal chewing tobacco tucked beneath his lower lip while he sipped his beers. He was the kind of guy

I'd only read about in books or seen in movies or heard crooned about in Southern rock songs. He was a rebel renegade, a man living on the road, a man with real problems and real-life experience.

More to the point, the hippie was everything I was not.

We had probably been sitting with the guy for thirty minutes when I felt a familiar pang of Christian guilt work through me. Now, when I say "Christian guilt" I don't mean that I felt bad for drinking beer or using profanity or for committing any other "sin" of the kind that often produces anxiety in young Christians. Rather, I felt guilty for what I *hadn't* done, for what I hadn't *said*.

I felt guilty that I hadn't shared my faith with him.

I tried to dismiss the thought. After all, I was (a) drinking beer and (b) having a good time. But no matter how hard I tried, I couldn't suppress this internal prodding. So as the hippie strummed along, I began concocting a scheme for how I could best pitch Jesus to him. When my plan was ready to go, I waited for him to finish the song he was playing.

"Do you know how to play 'Amazing Grace'?" I asked, my voice just loud enough to be heard over the song's final chord.

The hippie took a sip of his beer and then looked at me, his eyebrows furrowing. I glanced over at Kevin, who also had a bewildered look on his face.

"Yeah," I said, stammering a bit but trying to sound confident. "I mean, I've always loved that song."

The hippie scratched his head and then, smiling politely, said, "Nah, man. Don't know that one. But yeah, man, hell of a pretty song." He paused for a minute and then said, "How 'bout I play 'Let Her Cry' again."

Seriously, that's what he said. The dude *loved* Hootie.

Anyway, off he went, playing the song all the way through again, his voice getting louder at the line, "Let her go—let her walk right out on me." And while he was channeling Hootie front man Darius Rucker, I was thinking of how I could further engage him about faith.

This urgent need to talk about God might appear strange, but for me it was very normal. At that time in my life, it was a feeling that came over me nearly every time I spoke to a stranger.

It wasn't so much that I *wanted* to talk to the hippie about Jesus; I just felt *obligated* to do it. I began thinking of all the different things I'd been taught through the years about what happens when a Christian doesn't try to save someone's soul: how he has to answer to an angry God while the other person spends eternity in a lake of fire. In retrospect, it's as if I had constructed my entire theology based around the premise of a song from Nirvana's *Unplugged* album.

This need to pitch Jesus caused me a great deal of

internal conflict, because while I believed very much in Christian salvation, I also believed strongly in allowing people to live their own lives. Every ounce of me wanted to keep my mouth shut and not bother other people about heaven and God unless they brought it up. But then I would think about God watching over me, as though he were sitting on a cloud with a clipboard and taking note of my every action. I seemed to think I'd get "Jesus points" just for bringing him up, the way I used to get points toward a Pizza Hut prize for every book I finished in elementary school, whether I understood it or not.

It wasn't as if I wanted to talk to the hippie about Jesus because I felt I was in a position to discuss divinity with experience and confidence and compassion. I simply believed that God was keeping a tally of my wins and losses and that on Judgment Day I'd see all my numbers before me, written on a long scroll, like an athlete looking at his stat sheet after a game.

When I look back on many of these conversations, I see a lot of misguided arrogance in my thinking. It didn't occur to me that suggesting that someone conform to my ideas was a *huge* proposition. Rather, I thought that trying to talk someone into believing in Jesus was just something a Christian *did*, like praying every night and going to church every Sunday and voting Republican every fourth November.

So when the hippie finally finished playing his billionth encore of "Let Her Cry," I launched in with another request: "Do you know how to play 'How Great Thou Art'?"

The hippie scratched his face. "What's with all the Christian stuff, man?" he asked.

I looked over to Kevin, who seemed to be wondering the same thing.

Hesitantly, I said, "Oh, I don't know, man. Just, well, you know. I know it's not always the cool thing, but I'm a Christian, and that stuff's important to me." (I always assumed it was worth more points to God if I could make myself look like a martyr.)

The guy spit some chew into an empty beer can. "You really believe that stuff, man?" he said. His demeanor was very neutral, matching the tone of his question and the expression in his eyes.

"Yes," I said excitedly, my confidence growing, feeling as if I was going to be able to engage him. "I mean, yeah, man. I really do."

The guy took a sip of his beer. "Then how do you explain my girl running off with my baby. Why would God let that happen?"

I stammered a bit, not knowing how to respond. I figured the hippie's girl running off wasn't so much God's fault as his own, but I didn't want to tell him that.

"Or how do you explain all the evil in the world, you

know? Like, how do you explain the starving kids in Somalia—you know, crazy stuff like that?"

I remember sitting back and stroking my chin, pretending to be in deep thought but really wondering, what *was* happening in Somalia? (I was blissfully unaware of world issues.) Finally, despite knowing nothing about the issues he'd raised, I responded with some clichéd theological answer about "free will" that I'd been taught in school.

The hippie nodded, as if he was considering my argument. He strummed on the guitar a few times as he thought and then, looking up, said, "Well, if that's the case, then why did God give us free will in the first place?"

It was a standard theological question, but I was suddenly in deeper waters than my limited eighteen-year-old knowledge could stand in. The guy was smarter than me, and I knew it. However, not wanting to lose the debate, I decided to do what I always did when asked a pressing theological question for which I didn't have an answer.

I made one up.

Don't get me wrong: the answer I gave him *sounded* biblical. It just wasn't from the Bible, at least not that I was aware of. I merely said some flowery things about God that I thought made me sound both spiritual and smart.

I sat for what seemed like an eternity, waiting for the

hippie to respond. I remember he stared up into the stars for several long seconds and then finally looked at me. Very politely, he said, "Sorry, man. I just can't believe in that stuff."

Then he leaned over and spit some more Skoal into his beer can.

Not ready to give up, I tried taking a different route. I started talking about grace, about how no matter how many times we screw up God still loves us. Then I went on about forgiveness. Then I spoke about mercy. I'm pretty sure that before I finally gave up I'd given the hippie a detailed lecture on everything from Adam and Eve to the Fall of man to Jesus's favorite food to Mary Magdalene's hair color. I could tell the guy was getting annoyed, but I didn't care because by that point I was annoyed, too.

How could he not see the truth? I wondered. How could he be so blind?

We sat with the hippie only for another ten minutes, because I was so upset about losing the debate. That's how it always used to work when I was shot down trying to pitch Christian salvation: since my motivations were not pure, I always took the denial as a personal rejection.

When Kevin and I finally left the hippie that night, I remember having a thought that I'm ashamed to admit to now. I remember thinking that, one day, when the hippie was in hell, he'd remember our conversation and realize that I was right—that he should have listened to me.

It was in the following spring that I first heard the term *network marketing*. I was sitting in my dorm room trying to learn guitar (much to my roommate's dismay) when a young evangelist from my hall came barging in with a look of eagerness on his face. Now, it's important to note that, though this boy evangelist lived nearby, I didn't really *know* him. I had heard him speak at hall meetings a couple of times, about the "major ministry" God was performing through him, and I knew he was one of those young men from my Christian college who on weekends flew to churches around the country to "save souls." Still, we hadn't really had a conversation before.

Regardless, Boy Evangelist sat down in my computer chair, kicked his feet up on my bed, locked his fingers together behind his head, and told my roommate and me that he was "about to change our lives."

"Sounds fascinating," I said, turning my attention back to the guitar.

Boy Evangelist ignored my sarcasm. "I'm going to make you a millionaire in less than five years," he said.

I'll give him this: he was confident.

"How are you going to make me a millionaire?" I asked.

Boy Evangelist took his feet off my bed and leaned forward. "It's called Pre-Paid Legal," he said, his voice low and conspiratorial, like he was an actor delivering a key line in one of the Bourne movies.

"Pre-Paid Legal?" I repeated.

Boy Evangelist nodded. "I've already made a thousand bucks, and I've only been doing this for a week," he said.

Okay, I was intrigued.

"Plus," he said, "the beauty is that you make money off teaching *other* people to make money."

I scratched my chin. "Unpack that."

Boy Evangelist looked around, as if for a suitcase. "Unpack what?"

"*Explain*," I said.

"Oh," he laughed. "I've never heard that before. Unpack, that's funny. I'm going to use that. Anyway, here's how it works: you sign up to be a salesman for the product. Then you try to talk other people into selling the product, too. For every application someone under you turns in, you get a commission."

"Someone *under* me?" I said.

"Yeah, in your down line."

"My *down* line?"

"Yeah, the people under you."

"Have you ever heard of circular reasoning?" I said.

"No."

"Didn't think so."

"What is it?"

"Never mind," I said. "What's the product?"

Boy Evangelist scratched his face. "Well, it's legal insurance, but that's not the important part. The way you make your *real* money is by talking *other* people into selling it."

Now, obviously this sounds like the definition of a pyramid scheme, and anyone with half a brain would have shifted his attention right back to annoying his roommate with his guitar. But since I'm both (a) a moron and (b) a sucker, I was ready to sell some legal insurance.

"Let me get this straight," I said. "All I have to do is sign up to sell this crap, and then I go and talk a bunch of other people into selling it, too. Then I make money off of everything *they* sell?"

"Exactly."

"How do I sign up?"

"It's easy," Boy Evangelist told me. "I'll bring you the application. You pay $350, and then you start selling to everyone you meet."

I barely had that much money in the bank, but I went and got my checkbook.

Now, I am going to condense this story, so I won't get into the details of how greed and love for money turned Boy Evangelist into, arguably, the biggest pothead and boozer I've ever met. I won't tell you about the sketchy "pastor" named Nico, who served as network marketing mentor for Boy Evangelist and me. I won't tell you about how Nico taught us to lie and twist the truth when talking people into buying our product. I won't tell you about the numerous meetings and rallies I attended up and down the East Coast in hopes of learning more about selling my product. I won't tell you about the days I spent going door-to-door hocking legal insurance. I won't tell you about how I talked several of my good friends into buying my product by leading them to believe that I would make them millionaires. And finally, I won't tell you how I walked away from network marketing because I realized people were beginning to avoid me because they knew I was going to try to sell them something.

What I *will* tell you is the hook line I would use when trying to talk someone into becoming a member of my down line. When explaining how a "down line" worked, I would use this analogy (which, it's very important to note, I'd been taught in a Christian discipleship course years earlier):

"It's like in Christianity," I'd say to the prospective recruit. "Let's assume you save two people. Then those two people go and save two more people; then those two people go and save two more people. Eventually, there are people all over the world—hundreds, millions— who are saved just because of you. It's just like that with

Pre-Paid Legal. Only with Pre-Paid Legal, we're talking about money, not eternity."

Several years later I was at the after party for the final show of my season on *Survivor*. It was a really great time, a night for reuniting with all the people with whom I had spent such an emotional month and a half. I count that night as one of the top-five best times I've ever had.

About halfway through the party, my mother pulled me aside. "I just had the neatest conversation with Bobby," she said. Bobby is one of my good friends from the show who was part my original "young guy" tribe: a group that was comprised of four younger men.

"What'd he say?" I asked.

My mom took a sip of her drink. "Well, apparently on one of the first nights you guys had a talk about Christianity," she said.

I scratched my head, vaguely recalling that night. I remembered how, at that point in the show, we'd been on the island for only three days, and all I knew about Bobby was what he'd told me so far: that he was a rapper from South Central in Los Angeles and worked in video production with his brother. I had also gleaned a thing or two just by looking at him: he was an enormous bear of a man with tattoos all over his body.

What I didn't know was that he was a Stanford Law

graduate, a practicing attorney at one of the largest entertainment law firms in LA, and a man well read on matters of philosophy.

On this particular night, Bobby and I had drawn fire detail (which meant we were supposed to stay up around the fire all night and ensure that it didn't go out). Bobby, knowing I was a Christian, decided to launch into some pretty deep spiritual and theological questions.

Like I said, I remember the night but only vaguely. I don't really remember what he asked me about Christianity, nor do I remember my own words. I said as much to my mother.

"Well, apparently that conversation was important to him," she said, "because he came looking for me just to tell me about it."

"Well, what'd he say?"

My mother ran her pointer finger around the rim of her glass, thinking. "He told me that he was always going to remember you."

"Obviously," I said. "We starved on an island together."

"I know. That's what I said, too." My mother smiled. "But he told me that it was deeper than that. He told me that on the night you two discussed Christianity, you answered some of his questions in a way he'd never had a Christian answer him before."

"I did?" I said, shocked.

"Uh-huh," my mother nodded. "He said that he purposely asked you some really deep theological questions and that you, instead of trying to explain something no one can really explain, simply said, 'I honestly don't know. I just have faith.'"

My mother smiled again. "He told me that hearing you say that, and seeing how much you really believed it, meant more to him than any Christian trying to give an answer for something that, in this life, no one can truly answer."

As strange as it sounds, in that moment I thought back to my time selling Pre-Paid Legal. I remembered how, when a prospective buyer would ask me questions about my product, questions for which I didn't have the answers, I'd make something up. I recalled how dejected I felt when I realized that my friends were purposely avoiding me because they knew I was going to try to sell them my product. I remembered how it occurred to me that my approach to sharing my faith, as I tried to do with the hippie, was exactly the same as my approach to network marketing. I had turned Christian salvation into nothing different from a pitch for buying Amway or Cutco knives or Pre-Paid Legal.

And though it seems odd, I believe it was what I learned from my venture into network marketing that enabled me to give Bobby such a simple, truthful answer when he pressed about my faith. Had I never seen the connection between the way I tried to build a Pre-Paid Legal down line and my previous conversations about faith, I probably would have answered Bobby's questions by telling him all about free will and grace and Mary Magdalene's red hair, just like I did with the hippie years earlier. I would have made up some deep-sounding answers to try to appear smart and win the debate.

But here's what I am slowly beginning to understand about Christian spirituality: it's not a debate.

There is no argument—no words, no creed, no doctrine, no *nothing*—that is going to convince someone that the whole Jesus thing is real. Only the Spirit of God can do that. If God is not the instigator of the conversation, then trying to convince someone about faith is like throwing darts at a brick wall.

And, most important, pushing the point makes you come off like a self-righteous salesman.

I learned the hard way that people don't like being viewed as a sale, that they have a keen intuition for when someone is genuine and when someone is trying to sell them something.

Just like with network marketing, the ultimate agenda in pitching Christian salvation out of fear and guilt is to turn a human being into a sale. When the motivation for sharing faith is more about how it will affect the sharer rather than listener, then the sharer is not *engaging* God but, rather, is simply talking *about* Him.

I believe Christian salvation is a beautiful thing, and when I feel, deep within me, that God is leading me to discuss my faith with someone, I eagerly do it. But this kind of internal prodding isn't sparked by guilt or fear. Rather, it comes from compassion and love.

I've found that conversations about my faith most often materialize not because I broach the subject but, rather, because, as in the case with Bobby, someone grows curious about why the Christian faith is so important to me. And in those instances I simply try to express that while I can't prove God's existence, I wholeheartedly believe in it, and that it is this belief that colors the way I see the entire world.

One of the things I find so beautiful about the Bible are the stories of how Paul and the great Christian evangelists never spoke a word about Jesus or went into any new city to spread his teachings without first being prodded by the Holy Spirit to do so. In fact there are several passages in the Bible that describe how these early Christians' evangelistic plans were foiled because they acted on their own agendas rather than waiting for God's urging.

I believe God operates in this same way today: he leads us into relationships that aren't necessarily built around shared faith, but he will open the door for us to share our beliefs if and when it is his will. True to this idea, Bobby and I still have conversations about the

Christian faith to this very day, even though I've never once tried to pitch it to him. And though I have no idea where the hippie dude is today, I imagine that wherever he is he's playing the hell out of some Hootie and the Blowfish.

I'll Always Drive an Old Pickup

I recently bought an old pickup truck. I'm not talking about one of those new numbers with the big tires and the spiffy sports package and the sleek body style. I'm talking about a 1984 Dodge Ram, the kind that has been through four different owners, the kind that, if featured in a movie, would always appear on-screen while a song by the Eagles or Willie Nelson plays softly in the background. The truck is red and white, and I'm still feeling it out for a name. I was leaning toward Peppermint Pete, but then I realized that name was about as masculine as a boy's night at the ballet. So now I'm leaning toward calling it Red Auerbach, after the legendary Boston Celtics coach.

I got Red for two thousand dollars. Could I have afforded to make payments on a nicer car? Probably. Could I have found a "cooler" car? Sure. But Red has character. Red speaks of where I've been in my life and what I've been going through. Red reminds me of sitting on a deserted island on *Survivor*, wanting food, starving, realizing how much I have taken for granted in my life. Red reminds me of helping my parents move out of the house I grew up in, the house they'd planned to live in until their deaths, and into something more affordable. Red reminds me that I've bought into the Christian philosophy that we should "owe no man any debt other than to love one another."

Yeah, Red has character.

I grew up thinking that spending money was cool. Growing up, my sister and I always had the newest clothes, the newest video games, and the newest CDs. It felt like we were in a competition to stay ahead of the curve and have the latest fashions and accessories. I wanted them all.

But then I got old enough to understand why Seadog, my dad, didn't smile as much as he used to, why it seemed as if his spirit had been dragged behind the barn and gotten its butt kicked by Jack Bauer from *24*.

Debt is a vicious animal. It creeps up on a man while he's sleeping and coils around him like a python. But it doesn't squeeze immediately; for a moment it leaves him feeling snug and secure, creating a brief sense of pleasure. Then debt begins squeezing, and the man is gasping for air.

I see it everywhere I look these days. Everyone's in debt. Why?

There seems to be an unspoken societal paradigm to which we feel we are supposed to conform. No sooner have we received our college degrees than we suddenly find ourselves sucker punched by all sorts of unreasonable expectations and pressures. Next thing we know, we're dragging lead weights behind our designer shoes.

We feel we have to get a "real job"; we have to buy a house. We have to have a nice car and a big-screen TV (in case the neighbors come by). The problem is that we can't afford these things. But will we, the young people of generations X and Y, let that deter us? Of course not. Don't be foolish. We'll lease. We'll buy on a payment plan. We'll use *credit*.

I imagine a menacing red devil with pointy horns and a swirling, dark chocolate beard standing before his demon minions, pronouncing, "I have figured out how to get them, boys. It's called credit!"

Credit is a deadly seducer promising instant gratification while leaving us with an ever-growing mountain of debt that renders us incapable of enjoying what we've already purchased. Its hook is that it allows us a brief moment of vanity. Thanks to credit, we can buy flashy things we don't need, to impress people we don't care about.

I'm trying my best to be done with materialism, and I owe it to having finally figured out who Jesus is.

For years I understood the God of the Bible as being in

the business of financially rewarding those who diligently seek him. One can't totally fault me for this logic: in the last decade there has been a huge push in pop-Christian circles to paint God as some sort of Morgan Stanley portfolio manager who answers people's prayers for cash and success. With the phenomenal success of books like *The Prayer of Jabez*, and with wealthy pastors from megachurches seemingly representing proof of God's favor, it has become very easy for twenty-first-century Christians to indulge the idea of God as Santa Claus.

But as I studied the Bible more carefully, I began noticing that the Jesus portrayed in the Gospels was not the type of man who showed favoritism through wealth and material possessions. Instead the Gospels present the story of a man who was untroubled by possessions, a man who had no interest in accumulating money. Quite the contrary, the Jesus I read about proposed that his followers give willingly of what they had. He felt that *giving* wealth, not accumulating it, was the way to truly abide in worldly peace.

It was Jesus's lifestyle that led the apostle Paul to write to the church in Rome: "Owe no man any debt other than to love one another." I find this concept to be very inspiring. Whether or not you are of the Christian faith, this maxim is well worth analyzing.

I find it disheartening to watch people of my generation mature and begin making lifestyle changes dictated by vanity and materialism. I see people changing their friendships and choosing whom they will date or marry based on economic and social status. I know girls who aren't interested in guys who make less than a hundred grand a year, and I know even more who aren't willing to date a guy who doesn't drive a nice car (which I guess means they won't be dating me).

And it's definitely not just girls who make these kinds of choices. When I was living in Atlanta, trying to make it as an actor, I had a group of guys ask me to "hang" with them because they had heard I was a model. I wondered whether the invitation would be rescinded if I told them that I had only booked one job the entire time I was there. I would've asked them, but they had already jetted to the bathroom mirrors to make sure their Gucci shirts were exposing the proper amount of chest.

It's a gross system and I want out.

But who's to blame for all this? There's no question. I blame Lisa Turtle.

That's right. I'm fully prepared to place responsibility for all society's materialism issues on the shoulders of a *Saved by the Bell* character.

Lisa Turtle was the first fashionista I remember seeing on television. She was the first television character I remember whose underlying message was that shopping and constantly spending money was *cool*. These days all we have to do is turn on the TV to see this mad ideology taken to its terrifying extreme. If viewers of *Saved by the Bell* had been permitted to watch Lisa Turtle grow into an adult, marry, have children, and become a housewife, she would have been Mischa Barton's mom on *The OC*. (I'm not embarrassed to admit that I watched the first two seasons of *The OC* with heated fervor.) It's funny, but what's scary is that it's true. This type of transformation from lovable, fashion-obsessed teenage cutie to pretentious, pompous socialite is the reality of materialism and vanity: it creeps in and grabs us, and before we know it, it's turned us into wretches whose sole purpose in life is to acquire ever-higher social status.

In the last few years I've learned lessons that run counter to the preoccupation with money and status that's seen on television. I've observed the strength and solidarity of my family as it struggled against the odds—a group of people who realized they had nothing left except each other and were forced to pick up the pieces and start from scratch. I've learned that clothes are nothing more than the people wearing them, and that a house is nothing greater than the people living inside it.

Jesus had the right idea. His mission in life was to expose the hypocrisy and vanity of a world driven by selfishness and greed, and to promote the idea of offering undying love to other people. I've come to understand that it is only through the love of someone other than ourselves that we can actually love ourselves. And when all is said and done, is that not what materialism is all about, proving our self-worth? Maybe this is why we buy so much stuff, why we so often pretend to be people we aren't: we're trying to prove to ourselves that we are worthy of being loved.

This desire for approval is precisely the reason I love Jesus: the guy loves me exactly as I am. He doesn't care what I own or what others think of me; he loves me, not in spite of, but *because* I'm irreparably flawed and imperfect and poor and drive a pickup. He thinks my shortcomings are beautiful. This is a fascinating concept to me. Where in this society can you find someone who honestly loves you just as you are, not for the person you want to be, but the person you see in the mirror each night?

Ralph Waldo Emerson once wrote that "things are in the saddle and ride mankind." I think he's absolutely right. It's one of the reasons I've decided that I'll always drive an old pickup truck. It may not always be a 1984 Dodge Ram called Red Auerbach, but whatever the kind of truck, I know that I'll be driving it, and that it won't be driving me.

The Zack Morris Ethos

If I'm going to blame Lisa Turtle for society's materialism problems, then it follows that I should blame Zack Morris for my own issues with dating. Zack Morris's fictional life didn't just inform my ideas about what constitutes teenage coolness, it inspired pure imitation: I actually wanted to *be* Zack Morris.

I wanted Zack's life in its entirety. I wanted a best friend/nemesis like Slater. I wanted Screech to lionize me. I wanted a love-hate relationship with Mr. Belding. I wanted a brick-size cell phone.

And, *God*, how I wanted Kelly Kapowski.

To me, Kapowski was not just a cute television character, no mere sexy cheerleader for the Bayside Tigers. Rather, she was the early nineties incarnation of Aphrodite. Of Helen of Troy. Of Marilyn Monroe. Morris, for his part, was that era's Casanova. For these reasons, I used to cozy up to TBS every weekday afternoon with a sleeve of Pringles and study Zack Morris's life, like an athlete watching game film.

Zach was suave and witty, yet sensitive and empathetic. He was athletic and tough, but creative and kind. He never did his homework, and he was always late for class, but inexplicably he made a 1500 on his SAT and was (at least by the end of each episode) every teacher's favorite student.

Simply put, Morris was all things to all people, which I realized was precisely what made him loved by all the girls and envied by all the guys. Trying to duplicate these results, I set out to emulate Zack Morris in my own life.

However, as a wide-eyed adolescent I didn't realize the problem with being Zack Morris, which turns out to be a big one: the Zack Morris ethos suggests that one can cement his sense of self-worth through the adoration of women and the envy of men (or vice versa for ladies). In other words, Zack Morris's fictional life represents a very base idea: that true fulfillment comes from other people *wanting you*.

The Zack Morris dating mentality stresses that cozying up to one person for too long is bad, because you might get hurt the way Zack did when Kelly dumped him. To avoid this heartbreak, it suggests that you crush hard on someone for a while—even to the point of tricking yourself into believing you're really in love—but never commit to them. That way you are always free to move on to someone else, like Zack did when he started hooking up with Stacey Carosi at his Malibu Sands Beach Club summer job.

There is no end to the dating cycle in the Zack Morris ethos. *A* plus *B* never equals *C* because *A* doesn't want *B* to help him equal *C*. In the Zack Morris ethos, *A* sabotages the equation so that *B* is never a valid integer.

To extend this metaphor further: while we are always Zack Morris, or *A*, in our life's equation, *B* is always some model turned actress who appears for a three-episode story arc—someone who is exciting for a moment but irrelevant to our character's larger plot. And the tragedy of this equation is the sum it ultimately yields:

Zack Morris + never-ending string of three-episode romances = Jerry Maguire.

When we become so consumed with ourselves, so busy trying to prove our self-worth, so caught up in trying to look strong and smart and enigmatic and *independent*, without realizing it we become incapable of loving anyone else. All our energy is spent proving why other people should love *us*: the central problem Tom Cruise's character had in *Jerry Maguire*.

When I look around at my generation and its woes with dating, I realize that I am not the only person who has been misled by the Zack Morris ethos. Instead I see its terrible effects virtually everywhere I look. It is a stunning paradox really: our generation gripes about how we find our partners in relationships to be incapable of true commitment but then pat ourselves on the back by demonstrating how independent we are. It's as if we expect our partners to submit themselves fully to us but consider it an affront if they somehow suggest that we should do the same for them.

The best pop-culture example I can find to illustrate this phenomenon is Beyoncé Knowles's hit song "Irreplaceable." The lyrics are written from the perspective of a girl who has just caught her boyfriend cheating. In response to this, she warns him that she could quickly find somebody else just as good. She says:

> Don't you ever for a second get to thinking you're irreplaceable.

This leads me to wonder: if she really thinks her boyfriend is replaceable, why is she dating him? Isn't that kind of illogical?

Don't get me wrong; I realize that cheating is an offense that calls for an appropriately venomous response, but the nature of the infraction isn't the issue. The problem is the song's message. When one person says to another, "Don't think you're irreplaceable," the implication is that he should never drop his guard because someone else of equal or greater value is always waiting just around the corner.

It is a perfectly acceptable thing for a boss to tell an employee that he is replaceable, or for the band members of Creed to say this to Scott Stapp, but it should never be said by one member of a relationship to the other. Or even be thought about. If two people are truly committed, it should be because, at root, they find each other to be *irreplaceable*.

For the song's narrator to say something so confrontational suggests a very defensive nature, one that reveals how hell-bent our generation is on retaining an image of independence and individuality. It makes this otherwise irrelevant pop song so telling of our generation's approach to dating. The lyrics expose one of our deepest needs: to have other people realize how independent and desirable we are and to make them want us for this reason.

Not too long ago I went hiking in the mountains with the pastor of a neat little artsy church in downtown Greensboro. This pastor is a young guy, probably about thirty-five or so, and he is one of the coolest people I've ever met. In all honesty, I have a bit of a man crush on him. He's too suave and good-looking to be a pastor, and he's too articulate and wise to be only thirty-five. When

I'm talking with him, I find myself using big words (even if I don't know what they mean) and referencing obscure literature (even though I've never *read* any obscure literature). He's kind of like Dr. McDreamy from *Grey's Anatomy*, only he's an ordained minister, not a doctor.

Pastor McDreamy goes to the mountains every Tuesday. He says he likes to go up there so he can be alone with nature and meditate upon the Bible.

One Sunday after service, I told Pastor McDreamy that I would like to meet up for coffee. He surprised me by asking if I would rather go hiking with him instead. Like a smitten Meredith Grey, I jumped at the offer.

The following Tuesday, I found myself sitting with Pastor McDreamy on a cliff in central North Carolina, both of us staring down at a valley of trees that had just turned yellow-orange with the autumn. We sat there for about half an hour, discussing all kinds of things regarding faith and Jesus's life. Somehow our conversation soon shifted to the state of my own life. And in a strange bout of helpless vulnerability, I heard myself telling Pastor McDreamy all about my fear of commitment.

At this juncture, I was in a very tricky place with my girlfriend. She and I had been dating for about a year and a half, making our relationship by far the most substantial and meaningful one I'd ever been in. However, she was about to quit her job and was in the process of looking for new jobs in faraway cities.

And I wanted her to stay.

In fact, I wanted it more than anything I'd ever wanted. But I was having an extremely difficult time telling her this, because I knew that in asking her to stay I was, in effect, asking her to rearrange her entire life around *me*.

As I continued explaining my situation to Pastor McDreamy, telling him how scared I was of her leaving and how badly it would hurt me, I let it slip out that I have a fear of commitment.

"Why do you think that is?" he asked.

I sat back. "I honestly don't know."

"Is it that you think she'll cheat on you?"

"No," I said. "It's not about that."

"So then what's it about?"

"I don't know. I guess it's about a fear of finality or something, you know?"

"So are you saying that you're scared *you* will cheat on her?"

"No," I said. "That's not at all what I'm saying. I don't want to hook up with anyone else, and even if I did I wouldn't. It's just the knowledge that I never *can* that scares me."

"Go on," he said.

I scratched my chin. "It's just that, when I am in a relationship, I am very loyal. I don't flirt with other people and I don't cheat. And there is this part of me—this part of me that I wish wasn't there—that *likes* flirting, you know? That likes flirting because I enjoy knowing people like me. I know that's really shallow and vapid and embarrassing, but it exists. And I hate it."

"So you fear that by moving toward marriage, you will be starving your need to flirt?"

"Yes!" I cried. "I never thought of it that way, but yes; that's exactly what I mean."

Pastor McDreamy nodded. "But you love your girlfriend?"

"Yes, I do. I know I do."

"Well then, I can tell you what your problem is," he said.

I waited.

He stared at me intently. "You find your identity in trying to make people like you."

"What?" I said, totally thrown. "No, I don't."

"Yes, you do," Pastor McDreamy nodded. "And you want it as much from guys as you do from girls. You like knowing people respond to you; you like knowing they find you interesting and desirable."

I sat quietly.

He continued, "It's all very normal. This is one of the ways we as human beings feel a sense of self-value—by knowing people like us and want to be around us."

He paused, waiting for me to respond.

I nodded slightly but then looked down. I started chewing on my thumb, thinking. It was all pretty heavy stuff to be learning about myself. Epiphanies are never easy pills to swallow.

Finally, realizing I had nothing more to add, Pastor McDreamy said, "Subconsciously, you are scared to commit because you know that a real commitment will change the way you act toward the people around you . . . and you feel that people won't respond to the new you . . . and you feel like if you can't do something to *make* people respond to you, suddenly your life won't have meaning."

He paused before finishing, "You see, it's not really about your fear of committing to your girlfriend; it's about your fear of committing to yourself."

We left the mountains pretty soon afterward, and as we drove back to Greensboro, we talked more about all of this. When I finally got back home, I spent a great deal of time by myself, thinking about what Pastor McDreamy had said and trying to figure out what it all really meant.

Ultimately, I realized that he was right. He was telling me that I am scared of commitment because I am scared of accepting unconditional love. It's as if I feel I am not worthy of receiving love unless I am constantly doing something to get it. I make love about *me*. I am much more comfortable trying to win love than I am trying to accept it, because when I am winning love, I am putting on a stage show, but when I am accepting love, I am sitting back and letting the real me come out from hiding. And that's the crux of the problem: I am terrified of letting anyone see what the real me is like.

In an interview about a decade ago, the actor George Clooney famously said that, after having been married once, he would never get married again. Lately, I have started wondering at the amazing self-awareness that comment took. Because in making it, Clooney wasn't disparaging his ex-wife or the union of marriage but, instead, was indicting *himself*, saying that he didn't believe he was ever going to overcome his own selfishness.

This is a sentiment I feel we should all be able to relate to. It touches on a sad truth about human nature: we are all helplessly consumed with ourselves. Even if we aren't self-professed antimarriage people like Clooney, we are often too interested in promoting ourselves to provide a spouse or significant other with the love and affection they need. This can be true even of the people most vocal about how happy their relationship is or the people most adamant about wanting to settle down with someone. No matter our situation, we all have a base desire to use our relationship for self-gratification. In other words, to steal an idea from John F. Kennedy, when approaching relationships we typically ask not what we can do for our relationship but what our relationship can do for *us*.

Take for example the movie *The Notebook*.

Every female between the ages of eight and eighty fawned over this thing like it was the bible of dating. Consequently, Ryan Gosling's character, Noah Calhoun, became the Jesus standard by which all guys should be measured.

Meanwhile, most guys secretly liked the movie, too. We all choked back tears when James Garner and Gena Rowlands made out in the old-folks' home at the end, and then, when watching the credits roll, we made sure our significant others promised never to tell a soul that we'd wept like sissies. Years after the movie's release, we still haven't forgotten how cute Rachel McAdams's dimples were when Noah built her that house, and we still fantasize about yelling, "It wasn't over . . . it *still* ain't over!" as we catch her in midair and kiss her in the pouring rain.

Yes, thanks to Nicholas Sparks, all girls now pine for a guy like Noah Calhoun and all guys desire a girl like Allie Hamilton. What interests me about this is that guys don't spend more time wondering how *they* can be like Noah and, on the flip side, that girls don't spend more time wondering how *they* can be like Allie. To me this is a perfect example of our lopsided focus on how others can make our lives better as opposed to what we can do to improve theirs.

I think that this is what George Clooney was getting

at when he said he never wanted to get married again. He was saying that, while marriage is based on making a full commitment to another person, he cares too much about himself to make that commitment.

Which brings me back to Beyoncé.

Our entire generation shares Clooney's sentiment when it comes to relationships, and this idea is indirectly given voice in that Beyoncé song. We are all terrified of sacrificing our pride and our ego and our desire and our individuality. Therefore we commit halfway: we speak of commitment with our lips but hold back with our hearts. That way we never have to admit that we find someone irreplaceable. Should we ever get hurt, we can stand our ground and say, "You must not know about me. I could have another you in a minute."

To commit fully to someone, to do it the way it is *really* supposed to be done, means agreeing to put someone else's needs ahead of ours. We are, in effect, telling someone that, to us, they are irreplaceable, that we can't conceive of ever being without them.

And here's the hardest part: we have to *mean* it.

However, everything we have been taught as a generation runs counter to this. We have been indoctrinated with the Zack Morris ethos, the one that suggests that we are always supposed to be cute and charming and witty. Independent and resilient and unbreakable.

Always ready to seek self-gratification. Always prepared to promote ourselves to get it.

And what scares us, whether we are willing to admit it or not, is that a true commitment requires breaking ourselves of this mentality.

This is why true commitment is the ultimate sacrifice; not because we will be spending our lives with just one person, but because true commitment is built around abandoning our every impulse of self-protection. Much like Jesus's model of sacrifice, it requires us to love someone more than we love ourselves. And it requires our accepting someone else's unconditional love.

So when Pastor McDreamy told me I was refusing my girlfriend's unconditional love, it was like Mr. Belding showing Zack how to be a better man at the end of an episode. Pastor McDreamy was saying that for me to genuinely love my girlfriend, to commit to her fully, I had to allow her to love me, the *real* me—kind of like the Eagles suggest in that song "Desperado."

I'm finally beginning to understand it. I'm finally starting to realize that, in order to have a fully committed relationship with my girlfriend, I constantly have to give over every selfish desire I have. I have to admit how consumed I am by the need to feel wanted and important, and meanwhile I have to do everything I can to make *her* feel wanted and important. This is an ongoing learning process for me: one I have not come close to finishing.

It is difficult for me to shed the Zack Morris mentality. But I am trying very hard, because I don't want to end up like Jerry Maguire. And seeing as my girlfriend is my Kelly Kapowski, I am willing to do whatever it takes to make her feel irreplaceable.

On Being Dumped

I am a firm believer that there is no greater virtue than humility. I'm also a firm believer that there is nothing more humbling than a solid dumping. Therefore the following is a detailed list of my three most humbling experiences (in chronological order):

Case File No. 1:

Name: Madison Story
When: sixth grade
Where: Ferndale Middle School gymnasium
How: face-to-face
Soundtrack: "End of the Road" by Boyz II Men

I was in sixth grade when I started going out with Madison Story. In retrospect, I can't really understand why the chosen term for togetherness in middle school was *going out*, seeing as no couples I knew ever *went* any-where. Nonetheless, Madison and I had been "going out" for about two months (I think).

Madison Story was not my first girlfriend. My first girlfriend was Stephie Hall, who I "went out" with in fourth and fifth grades. But if memory serves me correctly, I ended that relationship, effectively kicking off my dating career at a solid 1–0.

The details of my relationship with Madison are a touch foggy now, but I do recall that we used to pass each other notes in math and social studies, and that she had a brother who was on my YMCA Midget League basketball team.

As far as I knew, things had been going along swimmingly for me and Madison, and I distinctly remember that we were both looking forward to the after-school dance coming up one Friday. (I used to get very excited about the four school dances each year. I went to them looking forward to the two slow songs the DJ would play, because those were the only occasions when I'd pry myself from the wall and dance with my significant other.)

When the big day arrived, I showed up at school bustling with excitement, ready to shake my tail feather. However, I soon discovered that my girlfriend wasn't sharing my enthusiasm.

Instead Madison cried the entire day. When the dance finally started, she stayed outside the gymnasium, in the common area, crying more. At different intervals throughout the dance, I went outside to check on her, only to find her weeping in the arms of various teachers and friends.

Now, when I say she was "crying," I mean she was a *wreck*. To this day, I don't know that I've ever seen anyone cry so hard (except for maybe those girls who don't get a rose on *The Bachelor*).

I was completely oblivious as to why Madison was so upset. Looking back, I probably should have been tipped off by the fact that everyone but me had been allowed into Madison's crying circle that afternoon. And by "everyone," I mean *everyone*. I'm pretty sure even the janitor and lunch lady were privy to the fact that I was about to get the ax. Blissfully ignorant to the cause of Madison's tears, I was not scared but, rather, annoyed. I kept checking my watch, hoping and praying that Madison would come inside before the final slow song was played.

Finally, about twenty minutes before the dance was scheduled to end, Madison made her way into the gymnasium. However, instead of coming to me, she went over and made camp in the corner.

Well, nobody puts Baby in a corner.

I made a beeline over to her just as the DJ started playing the final slow song: Boyz II Men's "End of the Road." (I swear to God, I'm not making this up. My first-ever experience of being dumped was set to the most gut-wrenching breakup ballad of all time.)

The lyrics picked up as I made my way to Madison.

"May I have this dance?" I asked, reaching for her hand. (I was very chivalrous at this young age. This was before I realized that chivalrous boys get dumped to songs like "End of the Road" in favor of boys who skip songs like "End of the Road" to go smoke cigarettes behind the school cafeteria.)

Madison, whose cheeks were stained black from running mascara, gave a slight nod. Taking my hand, she followed me to the dance floor.

Madison and I faced each other.

We made sure we were separated by at least two feet.

She swayed to the music.

I swayed (but since I have no rhythm, it was not quite to the music).

Nearly a minute went by without either of us saying anything, just swaying quietly to those haunting lyrics. Finally, I decided to pierce the silence.

"So what's wrong, Madison?" I said. "Why have you been crying all day?"

Madison looked at me with what I now know to be a look of pity. With a tear trickling out of her left eye, she whispered, "It's not you, it's me . . ."

Now, this was the first time that I'd ever heard "it's not you, it's me." So I didn't understand that those words really meant the exact opposite, that in truth what she was really saying was: "it's *totally* you, because . . . well, because I just don't like you. But I am too chicken to tell you this because I know it will hurt your feelings, and I want to be able to escape this mess without feeling responsible for anything."

Since I didn't know this, I believed her.

I ended our slow dance that day truly believing that it wasn't me, that it was Madison. Who knows, maybe this small piece of consolation was what enabled me to keep my tears at bay until the song ended.

I wouldn't find out until the next day that in truth I was being dumped for an eighth-grade boy who I knew smoked cigarettes.

I will say this: Madison never saw me cry that day (at least, not while we were dancing). But just after we parted ways, I crumbled. I sprinted straight to the far wall of the gymnasium where we had all placed our book bags and, very gracefully, did a swan dive into them. I then proceeded to cry unabashedly and indiscriminately, like the child I was. For the next ten minutes countless friends, classmates, and teachers came over to console me while I sat crying. I distinctly remember the phys-ed teacher, Coach Angel, telling me that there were "many fish in the sea."

His words were wasted; I wanted *that* fish.

I left school that day more wounded than I'd ever

been, so wounded that I didn't even realize how humiliated I should have been.

The next day I smoked my first cigarette.

Retrospective Analysis:

Embarrassment Level (scale of 1–10): 11
Lesson(s) Learned: (1) "It's not you, it's me" is a lie;
(2) Boyz II Men are sadists.

Case File No. 2:

Name: Andrea Powell
When: seventh grade
Where: my bedroom
How: over the phone
Soundtrack: "When a Man Loves a Woman" by
Michael Bolton

In the weird way that things work in middle school, Andrea Powell was Madison Story's best friend (at least I *think* she was. Regardless, I know they were close).

Andrea Powell had thick dark hair and copious freckles; she wore coordinated outfits from places like the Gap, and we lived on the same street (meaning, had I not been too chicken I could have ridden my bike to see her every day. However, this didn't happen a single time).

What I remember most about Andrea Powell are her braces: they were huge and seemed to dominate her entire face. Don't get me wrong: Andrea Powell was a very pretty girl, and, obviously, she was the one who ultimately dumped *me*. It's just that whenever I remember her, the very first thing that pops into my head is her braces.

I have very little recollection of my actual relationship with Andrea Powell (outside of the dumping). The one thing I remember definitively is that we went together to see the Flintstones movie (the one starring John Goodman) at our local theater, during which we held hands for so long that they began sweating.

Again details are sketchy, but I'm pretty sure Andrea and I "went out" together for a couple of months before things hit the rocks. I know for sure that it all fell apart just after she returned from spring break. I don't really remember where she went during that spring break, but it was somewhere in Europe. Wherever it was, it was more glamorous than Myrtle Beach, which is where I went with my friend Ryan Krull.

What I do remember is that Andrea came back from her trip acting *way* different from how she'd been acting when she left. Being too naive to consider that maybe she had met another guy, I assumed I was just imagining things.

A few nights later, after things hadn't changed, I

called her. I was sitting at my desk in my bedroom, the door closed and my heart pounding.

"What's wrong, Andrea?" I finally asked her.

A long silence, and then, "It's not you, it's me . . ."

Well, this time I knew better. I knew it was totally me.

I told her I understood and waited for her to hang up. Then I called my buddy Carson and tried to explain what had just happened, only for Carson, in turn, to explain to me that he already knew. At school that day, Andrea had told him that on her trip she had met an older guy named Jamie, and that she was planning to break up with me that night.

The next morning, on our way to school, my mother left me in the car while she walked my sister into her elementary school classroom. She always left the car running so that I could listen to the radio.

When my mother got back into the car, she found me crying to Michael Bolton's "When a Man Loves a Woman," which had just come on the radio. Looking back, I don't know what's more embarrassing: that my mother caught me crying or that I was crying to a Michael Bolton song.

Retrospective Analysis:

Embarrassment Level (scale of 1–10): 7

Lesson(s) Learned: (1) It's *never* a good thing when

your girl goes to Europe without you; (2) being the "older guy" is a huge advantage.

Case File No. 3:

Name: Jane Doe (as I'll call her because she has since enjoyed a moderate level of fame)
When: summer following freshman year of college
How: every way imaginable
Where: a lake in the mountains of North Carolina
Soundtrack: "Champagne High" by Sister Hazel

I met Jane Doe in Charlotte during the summer following my freshman year of college, while working a modeling job for Rack Room Shoes.

Now, when I say I was a "model," I use the word in the loosest sense possible. I booked *maybe* three jobs a year. Meanwhile, Jane Doe worked all the time.

I'm not going to sugarcoat it: Jane Doe was (and is) strikingly attractive. Not long after I met her, she moved to Los Angeles, where, as far as I know, she remains today.

I crushed on Jane immediately (as any heterosexual male would do). And, in a move that shocked me, she seemed to return the feeling. (This was likely because Jane was a year younger than I was, and I had the leverage of being the "older guy.") So after lots of shameless flirting, I finally gathered the courage to ask for Jane's number. Surprisingly, she gave it to me.

Unfortunately, Jane lived four hours away, in a tiny little mountain town called Cashiers. This killed my fantasies about the two of us spending the whole summer together.

Anyway, after a couple of weeks of talking on the phone every night, Jane invited me up to the mountains to visit her and celebrate the Fourth of July.

Obviously, I was stoked.

But I had one minor problem: my parents had sold my car while I was away at school, and I had no way to *get* there.

Enter my buddy Chris. (When it comes to the potentiality of meetings girls, Chris is ready to saddle up at any time.)

Chris, being the good friend he is, was willing to drive me to the mountains. So, a couple of days shy of the Fourth, we hopped in his jeep and made our way up to Cashiers, North Carolina.

All I remember about the long drive up is (1) we took a wrong turn and wound up in Tennessee, and (2) our favorite band, Sister Hazel, had just released its third studio album, *Fortress*, and Chris and I played the song "Champagne High" approximately seventy-seven times. Eventually, we found our way back into North Carolina and into the tiny town of Cashiers, a dot on the map that makes Mayberry look like Los Angeles.

Upon arriving, I called Jane and asked where we should meet her.

"Just meet me at the Ingles," she replied. "We'll be right down."

"Cool," I said, hanging up the phone.

"What'd she say?" Chris asked.

"Said they'd be right down."

"Who's *they*?" he asked.

I shrugged. "Maybe a friend."

"Yeah, dawg," Chris said, a huge smile spreading across his face. "She better be hot."

Well, it turns out I was exactly right: Jane was coming down with a friend. Only it was not just a "friend" but, rather, her on-again, off-again boyfriend, a dude with a strange name and big pointy ears like Mr. Spock.

I would find out later that Jane and Spock had been on-again, off-again for a couple of years, and that Spock's family had a summer house on the lake. Apparently, he'd just gotten into town that day.

Jane didn't tell me the truth about her relationship with Spock until the next day, leaving me to fill in the blanks for myself. So at first I figured Spock really was just a "friend." But then, when we got to the lake and went out on Jet Skis, something seemed amiss.

Maybe it was how she jumped on the back of *his* Jet Ski, only to spend the rest of the afternoon riding around the lake and hugging him from behind. Or maybe it was when we finished up at the lake and decided to go to Subway for a sandwich, she hopped in his car instead of into Chris's jeep.

Or maybe it was simply when I saw them making out later that night in his bedroom.

Regardless, my next two days were spent bouncing from one epic humiliation to another. Here are just a couple of the highlights:

1. *Mr. Spock patiently teaching me how to tie up a boat because I didn't know how (while Jane looked on and laughed at my ineptitude).*
2. *Jane and Mr. Spock waking up early to go for a six-mile run while Chris and I were left watching television with Jane's parents.*
3. *Jane and Mr. Spock taking the boat out for a romantic late-night cruise while Chris and I were left playing cards at Spock's house with his older brother.*
4. *Jane making Chris and me go to church with her while Spock got to sleep in.*
5. *Spock coming over to Jane's house to see me and Chris off, and holding Jane around the waist as he shook our hands good-bye.*

Why Chris and I didn't just pack up and leave on the first day, I honestly don't know. Obviously, it would have been the logical thing to do. Maybe it was my pride. Or maybe I'm just a closet masochist. Either way, even though this was not technically a *dumping*, it was quite possibly the most humbling *dissing* of all time.

Retrospective Analysis:

Embarrassment Level (scale of 1–10): 100
Lesson(s) Learned: (1) How to tie off a boat; (2) big ears give you even more leverage in picking up chicks than being the "older guy."

So, as clearly evidenced, being dumped is a fantastic way to learn true humility. For those of you who have yet to experience a true dumping (and are also interested in becoming a more humble person), you should really look into it. I *highly* recommend it.

Lost Just the Same

All of them . . . constructed at infinite cost to themselves these Maginot Lines against this enemy they thought they saw across the frontier, this enemy who never attacked that way—if he ever attacked at all; if he was indeed the enemy.

—John Knowles, *A Separate Peace*

I hate to admit this, but there was a time when I was scared of black people. I was eleven years old, and about to make the jump from elementary school to middle school. Frankly, I was terrified about it. And, if memory serves me correctly, it wasn't just me who felt this way: *all* the students from my 95 percent white elementary school were just as frightened. For most of us, this wasn't because we grew up in racist families (at least, I know for me it wasn't). Rather, it was simply that we had a profound fear of that which was different from us. In other words, we had a limited understanding of what black people were actually *like*. All we knew about black people we'd gleaned from early nineties movies and television. Therefore we assumed that every black person had the hardened personality of Tupac Shakur's character Bishop from *Juice* and was as quick mouthed and athletically dominant as Sidney Dean in *White Men Can't Jump*. We also knew, because of these movies, that if the black kids were like Wesley Snipes's Dean, we were like Woody Harrelson's nerdy character Billy "Ho" Hoyle. I remember it being a very daunting prospect to consider spending every day around people who were, quite obviously, so much tougher and cooler than I was.

It was with this mentality that I arrived for my first day at Ferndale Middle School. I remember being full of trepidation as my mother dropped me off in the parking lot, hugging me good-bye and telling me how much she loved me. I can still see her minivan disappearing around the corner, my metaphorical lifeline being severed. I saw several familiar faces from my previous school, standing around waiting for the bell to ring, and I quickly joined their circle, knowing instinctively that there was safety in numbers. When the bell rang, we all made our way to our respective homeroom classes. Luckily, one of my old school pals was in my homeroom, so together we found the classroom fairly easily.

Once inside, I remember scanning all the faces, trying to figure out who I knew and who I didn't, trying to determine who was cool and who was not. Homeroom lasted about fifteen minutes, and then it was off to first period. I had checked with everyone I knew, but none of my friends had first-period gym like I did.

I was on my own.

Looking back on that first day, I have no idea how I got lost upon leaving homeroom. The path from that classroom to the gymnasium was not at all complex. In fact it was a pretty direct shot. Still, I found myself lost, wandering the halls of Ferndale long after the tardy bell had rung. I remember trying not to panic, telling myself that only wimps would cry over getting lost at school. I willed myself to keep the tears at bay.

I had been wandering the halls for about ten minutes when I saw Antoine.

He was black.

He had on a heather gray T-shirt.

He had a glow about him, one that made his smile show in his eyes.

And, most memorably, he had a rattail that hung at least three solid inches from the back of his head.

He saw me standing awkwardly in the middle of the hall, looking both directions like a kid scared to cross the street. "What you looking for?" he said, making his way over to me.

It was terrifying how much I wanted to impress this person with the rattail. I puffed out my chest, trying to think of how a cool person would respond. "Oh, I don't know," I said, trying to sound carefree. "You know, I just . . . Well, I don't really know where I'm going."

The boy smiled at me again. "Yeah, me neither."

I studied him. He seemed completely at ease with being lost, so I tried to adopt his cool demeanor. I noticed that he was wearing his backpack with only one strap over his shoulder, so I casually slipped one of my straps loose. "So, where you headed?" I asked.

"PE," he said.

"Me too," I exclaimed, a bit too excitedly.

"Cool," he said. "What's your name?"

"Austin."

"I'm Antoine," he replied. "I just asked some teacher back there which way to go for the gym, and she said to go through that door." He pointed ahead.

"All right," I said, following him as he began walking. "I mean . . . that's cool."

We spent the next couple of minutes chatting as we worked our way toward the gym, Antoine casually commenting on things and me nodding vigorous assent to anything he said. He asked me about my old school and then told me about his. We realized we liked the same sports. We liked the same athletes. And when we finally made our way into the gym, nothing did more for my confidence than walking in with Antoine. I didn't know whether he was nearly as moved by our interaction as I was, but an emboldening feeling stirred in me: he was my new friend. And just as I started putting on the gym clothes we were handed, I had an epiphany that would stay with me forever: my new friend and I were not so different after all.

One day, eight years later, Antoine told me he had enlisted in the military. I will never forget that moment: late October 2000; he and I standing in the middle of a small street in Chapel Hill; my mouth opening to speak, but no words coming out. I remember glancing down, studying the wet autumn leaves scattered across the pavement.

"You're serious, aren't you?" I finally managed.

Antoine nodded.

I kicked at a leaf with my shoe, thinking. I was incredibly moved by his bravery, but I was scared to death for him. Up until this point, none of my close friends had enlisted in the military. "Are you sure this is what you want?" I said.

Antoine scratched his head. "No," he said. He stood pensively for a second and then added, "But for the first time in my life, I feel like I'm making a decision for *myself.*"

We had remained close ever since that first day of middle school when he and his rattail had shepherded me to my first-period class. Over those next eight years our whole group of friends had managed to remain close, despite the fact that, upon graduation, we had all opted to go to different colleges. As Antoine was telling me about his enlistment, we were on fall break, and we had all met up at UNC–Chapel Hill. At this point, Antoine had recently left the college where he'd been playing football. For the previous several months, he had been trying to decide what he wanted to do with his life: whether he wanted to go to another college or whether he wanted to stay in High Point and get a job. Until this moment, I'd never heard him mention anything about becoming a marine.

"How about you?" he asked me. "You still hate soccer?"

I nodded.

"Think you'll transfer?"

I chewed on my fingernail, thinking about how long I'd been complaining about playing college soccer. I had grown increasingly disillusioned with the sport in the last year and had been talking of transferring schools for quite a while. I glanced up to the porch where several of our friends were gathered.

"I don't know," I said finally, looking back at him. "Some days I think I will, and then other days I wonder if I'd regret it."

Antoine stood silently.

"You know," I continued after a pause, "it's like I have all of these reasons for wanting to leave. But then, I have just as many for wanting to stay."

Antoine gave me a serious look, as if he completely understood what I was saying. He patted my shoulder. "Come on, let's go grab a beer."

It wasn't until several minutes later, as he and I sat sipping Busch Lights in some stranger's house, that I realized Antoine *did* completely understand what I had been saying, because he felt the same way—confused.

Uncertain.

Scared.

Lost.

Sometime between that fall break and the subsequent Christmas, I went on one of my major Jesus highs. I began reading my Bible about a thousand times a day, regurgitating the information I'd processed to anyone willing to listen. And by the time I got back to college for the beginning of spring semester, all I could think about was Jesus. I remember lying awake in my dorm room for hours, reading my Bible, losing myself in the wonderings of people like Paul, Peter, and John—people whose lives exuded Jesus in every way.

Around this same time, Antoine left for boot camp.

He had been away for many weeks before I finally got around to writing him. This is something I struggle with: because of my unyielding selfishness I am horrible about keeping in touch with my friends. I often go months without calling friends, *best* friends, because I am too consumed with my own world to take a few minutes to reach out to them. It's as if I consider it an inconvenience to have to talk on the phone or write e-mails, so I end up alienating people I genuinely care about.

When I finally *did* sit down to write Antoine a letter, it wasn't one born of obligation. Instead it was sparked by a stirring in my spirit, a feeling that I should reach out to him, not just with updates and well wishes, but with words of Christian encouragement. I found this a very strange prodding because, while Antoine and I had been friends for a decade, we had only had a handful of discussions regarding Jesus and Christianity. Antoine came with me to church once, and I remember there was one night, early in college, when he and I and our buddy Mike were really drunk on the back patio at my parents' house, and we discussed Jesus and the explosive success of those *Left Behind* books. But outside of that, Antoine and I didn't really have a track record when it came to talking about Christianity.

Still, as I began considering the words I wished to send him that day, the words I hoped would give him strength and encouragement as he braved boot camp, I found myself, almost against my will, scribbling thoughts about Jesus. I told him that I wasn't sure whether he believed in Jesus, but that I hoped he did. I told him that, just before Christmas, I had been feeling empty, lost, and that revisiting my relationship with Jesus had provided me the peace I had been craving.

After I dropped the letter off at the university's post office, I felt a growing concern that I had gone too far, that I should have stuck to the basics—told him I missed him, asked him what boot camp was like, told him how I was still torn about whether I would leave school. Or maybe I should have talked about something "cooler," like hot girls or sports or beer. I walked around like that for the next few days, wondering if he had received the letter and whether it had offended him. So, about a week later, when I received an envelope posted from Paris Island, South Carolina, with Antoine's name on it, my heart skipped. I carried the letter back up to my dorm room, where I could read it in privacy. I sat down in my computer chair, right next to the window, the sun pouring through the blinds and making the envelope glow. Timidly, I opened it.

Antoine began his letter by thanking me for writing, telling me how receiving mail from his mother and his friends was the main thing keeping him going. He wrote about how hard boot camp was, how it was designed to push each person to his breaking point. He told me that he had never been through anything like it, and that I couldn't imagine how wearing it was. And then, finally, he addressed my comments about Jesus.

I wish I still had Antoine's letter so I could include it here, as my recollection of his words will surely cheapen the beauty and depth of what he wrote. But since I don't, I will have to paraphrase.

Antoine said that, a week earlier, he had reached out to Jesus. It had happened just after a voluntary chapel service; what the military chaplain said had really spoken to him. Antoine wrote that he had felt overcome with emptiness, with a feeling of being lost, and that everything the chaplain said related to what was going on inside him, especially that accepting Jesus meant not having to go through life alone. Antoine said he liked that idea, because he wasn't sure he could get through boot camp on his own. He told me that he *did* know the peace I wrote to him about, because he'd just experienced it.

It's been nearly a decade since I received the letter from Antoine saying he believed in Jesus, and it has been nearly two decades since I found refuge in his friendship. All these years later, we remain close.

Today I'm an adult inching my way toward thirty, and I am finally beginning to understand what I didn't as a sixth grader, and what I still didn't as a college sophomore: that all human beings are fundamentally the same. That we are all, at our core, driven by the same two forces: the fear of being lost and the hope of finding redemption. Whether we are children lost in a crowd or young adults trying to figure out what to do with our future, whether we are vexed by poor self-image or concerned about where we might spend eternity, we are all experiencing the same feeling: that of being lost. And all of us, in our most vulnerable moments, can find redemption only through the love of another.

Some time ago, I was at a *Survivor* event in New York, and I was talking to my brilliant friend Shane about how I could best handle a situation with my girlfriend. Shane looked at me very seriously and said, "Ask her how you can make her feel safe."

I looked at him curiously.

"That's what we all want, bro," he explained. "We just want to feel *safe*."

It was probably the most profound advice I've ever heard.

Because it's true.

As human beings we constantly feel vulnerable, whether we're willing to admit it or not, and we depend on others to make us feel safe. It's one of the main reasons I love Jesus: believing in him makes me feel secure.

It seems to me that when we are young we seek safety and validation from our friends, our peers, our parents. As we move toward adulthood, we begin realizing how few people we can *really* depend on; how fickle human nature really is; and how, by relying on other people, we leave ourselves completely open and vulnerable. At this point we begin internalizing, seeking security within ourselves, constantly telling ourselves that we are strong enough to go it alone: that we are *independent.* But eventually most of us reach a point where we are forced to admit that we only feel validated and secure when we have the love of someone else. And that's when many of us finally look to God: when we realize that we can't do it alone, and that his offer of unconditional love is, in fact, what we've been seeking all along.

Looking back, it seems ridiculous to me that, had we met on different terms, I might have been intimidated by Antoine, that I might have feared him simply because his skin was different from mine. I sometimes look at our crazy world and wonder why the seeds of prejudice still exist, why so many people can't see the folly in such thinking—why some people fear those of a different ethnicity, those of a different socioeconomic standing, those of a different religion.

Thinking about this problem saddens me, and I find myself lamenting how complex the fear of others really is, how difficult this type of fear is to overcome.

But then I think about that scared little boy pacing the halls of his middle school. I think about that other little boy, the boy of a different stripe, walking up to him and offering him a disarming smile. I think of how both boys admitted to each other that they were lost, how that admission helped them figure out that they were headed to the same place. And I begin wondering if overcoming fear isn't very complex at all. I begin wondering if maybe all we need to do is admit to each other how vulnerable we often feel. How, more often than not, all we really want is to feel safe.

And then I begin wondering if maybe, just maybe, by simply admitting to one another that we all feel lost, we will finally realize, just as those two little boys did, that we are all headed in the same direction.

Math Genius

When I was in middle school, I fantasized about getting suspended. My logic was that if I could just get suspended it would do wonders for raising my street credibility. This was in that curious period of time when making good grades suddenly (and inexplicably) became a bad thing, and misbehavior became a barometer of social acceptance. Don't get me wrong; I was generally liked in middle school, insomuch as I didn't go to school scared of beatdowns or getting stranded without a lunch table.

But I knew I wasn't *cool.*

Cool was a designation reserved for those who smoked cigarettes and flunked tests, for those who were allowed to watch *In Living Color* and who knew how to use the f-word as several different parts of speech. People who got in fights at school were cool. People who stole porn from their fathers' closets were cool. People who read all fifty-six Nancy Drew books of their own volition were hopelessly *not* cool.

In order to cement a cool persona, I concluded that it would require doing something dynamically and profoundly bad. This presented me with a slight dilemma, as I was far too much of a wimp to generate any legitimate badness. I couldn't flunk tests because I cared too much about my final grade, and I couldn't get in fights because I knew I'd lose. I couldn't smoke cigarettes either, because I'd tried that already and knew the end result would involve me hugging a toilet.

This left only one viable option: suspension.

Therefore I wholeheartedly pursued a school-sponsored vacation, employing every ounce of blatant rebellion I could muster. Unfortunately, very soon into my quest I realized that I simply didn't have the innate talent to get into serious trouble in public school. My intentional in-class napping paled in comparison with my classmate calling our teacher a "fat ass bitch." Likewise, my habit of showing up late for class didn't quite elicit the same reaction as my peer who was selling weed from his locker.

How could I possibly compete with behavior like that?

As middle school came to a close, I grudgingly came to grips with the fact that I, while certainly not an exemplary student, would never be a rebel. I just didn't have what it took to be cool.

But then I transferred into a Christian high school.

I feel I should explain the reason for this move. It wasn't that my parents wanted me to have a Christian education or that the public schools were becoming too rough. Rather, it was simply that the local Christian school had a nationally recognized soccer program, and, as a soccer player, I could benefit from it. So I left everything I understood about public school and its social code and plunged into the Christian alternative— where I realized something very quickly: one could get in trouble for just about anything.

While in-class napping was merely cavalier behavior in public school, it was downright inexcusable in Christian school. Whereas my showing up late for class was met with nothing more than a sigh in public school, here it quickly earned me after-school detention. Suddenly, I was in a place where *crap* was a legitimate cussword and where drinking beer was tantamount to armed robbery.

Within my first week in Christian school I realized that, while I had been incapable of getting noticed for my indiscretions in public school, I was now incapable of hiding them. No matter what I did, I got in trouble. I had never been sent to the principal's office in public school, but by my third week in Christian school I had memorized all the photographs on the principal's desk.

In order to combat my newly troublesome behavior, my teachers organized a monthly meeting with my parents to discuss my "progress." (Translation: the teachers sat around me in a circle, taking turns bemoaning my classroom antics and using the words "waste of potential.")

In all fairness, I must concede that many of my teachers' gripes were legitimate. I had become a real slacker and didn't care about my grades nearly as much as I once had. I had become too preoccupied with trying to win the role of class clown to spend too much effort on my studies. In retrospect, I imagine there was a good measure of truth to my teachers calling out my wasted potential.

However, I was full of indignation about getting in trouble for something as mundane as late homework or as ridiculous as pop-kissing my girlfriend at my locker. I knew that the things I was getting in trouble for in Christian school wouldn't be given a second thought in public school, and each time we left one of these progress meetings I'd tell my parents as much. Shockingly, my parents agreed with me.

That was, until I got caught cheating on a Bible test.

Now, I know how bad that sounds, and I'm not going to try to justify it, because it *was* bad. Worse still, it wasn't the only time I'd ever cheated; it was simply the only time I'd gotten caught. I had developed a cheating habit way back in elementary school, where I learned how much easier it was to look at my neighbor's paper than to spend hours studying at home.

I'll never forget the fear that seized me when my Bible teacher walked over and whispered that I should follow her outside. I felt tears nipping at my eyes (further evidence that I was never cut out for true coolness), and when she asked me if I'd been cheating, I ducked my head in shame.

Minutes later, I was in the principal's office yet again. Only this time I knew I'd done something truly bad, something about which my parents were going to be legitimately pissed. And because this was late November, I could only imagine how my punishment would affect my Christmas vacation.

When I got home that afternoon, I got the verdict: I wouldn't be *having* a Christmas vacation.

"No, I got the *second* one right," I heard my buddy Chase say as I sat down at my usual table in the cafeteria.

"You got the second one right?" our friend Brian responded. "I didn't have a clue how to do that one. I got the third one right."

Chase cackled. "Then who got the *first* one?"

"I think it was Mary."

It was our first day back from Christmas vacation and I was actually happy to be at school, seeing as I had been under house arrest through the entire break.

"What are you guys talking about?" I asked. I opened

my lunch sack and began pulling out the contents one at a time.

"Some test we had to take in math last period," Chase said. "We have some new teacher because Mrs. Wilson went on maternity leave."

"We already have a test in that class?" I asked.

"Oh, that's right," Chase said. "I forgot you have the same class next period. Yeah, there's a test."

I panicked. "On what? How can there be a test when we haven't even been in school?"

"Relax," Chase said. "It's not for a grade. The new teacher is just giving some test to see how smart everyone is."

"Huh?"

Chase nodded. "I know. Seemed strange to all of us, too. It's only got four questions on it, and they're, like, impossible. No one in our class got more than one right."

"Ah," I said, finally comprehending. "So that's what you were talking about when you said you got the second one right."

Brian piped in. "Yeah, and *I* got the third."

I took a bite of my sandwich. "You're sure it's not for a grade?"

Chase nodded. "Yeah, she told us right off the bat. Like I said, she just wants to see how smart we are."

"I imagine the zero I get will really impress her then," I said.

Chase snickered. "Nah, I bet you'll get at least one right."

Brian's face suddenly brightened. He looked at Chase. "Dude, why don't we tell Austin the answers we already know? Can you imagine the new teacher's face if he gets *three* of them right?"

Chase cackled, immediately turning to me. "Dude, she is going to think you're a genius."

Before I knew it, Brian had walked over and asked our friend Mary what the answer was for the question she'd gotten right. Then he and Chase told me the two answers they knew. Suddenly, without my solicitation, I knew three of the four answers on the test I was about to take.

"Guys," I said, my face serious, "I really don't know about this. I mean, I'm just about to get ungrounded. I can't get in trouble again—"

"It's not cheating," Brian interrupted. "The test isn't even for a grade. It's just some throwaway test to see how smart you are."

"You're sure?"

"Positive," Chase said.

I sat quietly for several seconds, thinking. "Okay," I said finally. "What are the answers again?"

Less than an hour later I was sitting in math class, listening as the new teacher timidly introduced herself and explained that she was filling in for Mrs. Wilson until she came back from maternity leave. Then she told us to clear off our desks.

"I'm passing around a test," she said as she began handing out the papers. "But it's not for a grade."

For the next thirty minutes the room was filled with the rare silence of students hard at work. About ten minutes later, several students began turning in papers. Each time one of the students got one right, the new teacher announced the achievement to the class. However, just like in Chase's and Brian's class, no one got more than one question right.

At around the forty-five minute mark, I finally walked my paper to the front. I stood back and watched the teacher's face as she began looking it over.

She nodded slightly after checking my first answer.

She bit her bottom lip after checking my second answer.

She held her breath after checking my third answer.

Then, much to my surprise, she *erupted* after checking my fourth answer.

"You got them *all* right," she half whispered, her eyes drunk with astonishment.

"I *did*?" I stammered. It had never crossed my mind that I might actually get the fourth answer on my own merit.

"Class!" the new teacher suddenly exclaimed, standing from her seat.

Everyone stopped what they were doing and looked to the front, where I stood uncertainly beside the new teacher.

She whispered into my ear, "What is your name?"

"Austin Carty," I stammered.

The new teacher looked back to the students. "Class, it is my honor to tell you that Austin Carty has gotten all four answers right!"

I watched each student in the class immediately shoot a curious look to someone else, a silent exchange that communicated an unmistakable thought: how did *he* get all four right?

When I left school that day, I was a hero. Not just to the new teacher but to the entire student body. Word of my accomplishment traveled the hallways at a scandal-like pace. By the time I was in my car heading home, every student in the school knew of my mathematical genius.

About three weeks later I was sitting in the middle of one of my monthly progress meetings. As usual, my parents were right beside me. However, unlike all the previous meetings, this one was an all-around lovefest. I had been doing everything I could to get sprung from being grounded, and thus fully applying myself at school during the last month. Consequently, every one of my teachers was heaping praises upon me. It was as if with each passing teacher's report I could feel my punishment subsiding.

When the first tear trickled from my mother's eye, I knew the grounding was over.

After the last teacher had spoken, the school guidance counselor, who had never before been part of one of these meetings, stood up. Until this point, it hadn't occurred to me how strange her presence was.

"This has all been fantastic news," the guidance counselor said. "It just confirms everything we have suspected about Austin."

My father nodded. My mother began crying again.

"But . . . I am happy to say that I have the best news of all!" she continued eagerly.

I began racking my brain. What else could there be?

The guidance counselor paused, taking a deep breath as if the news were so exciting that even she could hardly contain herself.

I sat forward in my seat. Beside me, I saw my mother grip my father's hand.

"Last month," the guidance counselor began, "Austin and the rest of our students took part in the ACSI Math Competition."

Math competition? I thought. What math competition?

"Now," the guidance counselor continued, "this competition is a four-question test that is administered by over five hundred Christian schools across the country."

Oh no . . .

The guidance counselor paused. She bit her lip as if to keep herself from crying. I felt my mother leaning forward in her seat beside me, as if preparing to use physical force if the woman didn't hurry up and finish her thought.

"And I'm proud to announce," the guidance counselor concluded, "that our very own Austin Carty, from Wesleyan Academy, was one of only four students across the country to get all four ACSI math questions correct!"

Oh God . . .

I looked to my mother, who was now crying harder than I'd seen her cry since Macaulay Culkin's character died in *My Girl*. Meanwhile, my father looked genuinely shocked. Around us, my teachers took to their feet and gave me a standing ovation.

"Now," the guidance counselor said, trying to bring the room back to order, "on to the logistics of this. We are going to make a huge banner to hang outside the front office to announce Austin's achievement. Then, of course, we'll call all the local newspapers and make sure they run a story about it. I think we may even be able to get him on the local news."

She paused. "But even if we can't, one thing is certain. Austin is a math genius."

• • •

I went to bed that night with my conscience as heavy as lead. It felt good being considered a genius, but I couldn't shake the nagging truth that I wasn't a genius at all. It was a big lie. I was no more a mathematical prodigy than I was a trapeze master or an ob-gyn.

That night I dreamed of being interviewed on the local news and fumbling the answer for a math question as simple as twelve times three. In the dream, the news anchor doubled over in laughter and had to go to a commercial break to regain her composure. I woke up sweating.

First thing the next morning, an announcement was made over the intercom alerting the student body of my outstanding achievement. Less than an hour later, the phone rang in my first-period class. It was the principal asking my English teacher to have me report to his office.

I took my time getting there.

When I finally opened the principal's door, I saw the new math teacher sitting beside him. On the principal's desk was my copy of the ACSI math test.

"Close the door behind you," the principal said.

I did as I was told, then took a seat.

"Now, Austin," the principal began. "About this ACSI test. We've had some students complain that you may have had some help getting—"

"Yeah," I said, interrupting him. "I can't take this. I cheated."

Less than an hour later, I was finally enjoying the school-sponsored vacation I had fantasized about years earlier. Ironically though, I didn't even *want* the suspension anymore. I no longer wanted the students to think I was a rebel. I wanted them to think I really was a math genius.

Two years later, with my genius moment far behind me and graduation imminent, I learned that I was one of only seven students in my entire graduating class who would not be wearing a shawl for either National Honor Society or Beta Club. When I found out, I was livid. I felt snubbed: my grades were certainly good enough, and I had a decent list of extracurricular activities.

My English teacher was the sponsor for both clubs, and after school I marched into her classroom and demanded she give me a reason for the snubbing. I had an entire list of arguments prepared to bolster my case.

But I wasn't prepared for her reaction.

She very calmly stared at my reddening face, placed her hands on my shoulders, and softly said, "Austin, you cheat in my class *all* the time."

"I . . . what?" I stammered. I'd had no idea she was aware of how often I cheated.

"Do you really want to make an issue of this?" she said.

I ducked my head. "No, I suppose not."

My teacher nodded. "Good. I'll see you tomorrow."

My English teacher, whom I must tell you I *adored*, then walked out of the room. Stunned, I stood frozen in the middle of the classroom, trying to get a grip on what had just happened. She knew I'd been cheating the whole time?

I was just about to leave when I saw, in the corner of the room, a pile of bright gold National Honor Society shawls. So what if I cheated a little bit, I thought. I deserve it just as much. My grades are just as good as everyone else's. So I walked over to the pile, stuffed one of the shawls in my pocket, and left the room.

When graduation came a couple weeks later, I sat with my crimson robe completely unadorned, but with a National Honor Society shawl sitting in my pocket. And when I got to college, I openly told people that I had been a member of the National Honor Society. They all believed me.

But, then again, why wouldn't they, when I had the shawl to prove it?

In Khaled Hosseini's best-selling novel *The Kite Runner*, the protagonist's father says something very insightful to his young son:

There is only one sin, only one. And that is
theft. Every other sin is a variation of theft . . .
when you tell a lie, you steal someone's right to
the truth. When you cheat, you steal the right
to fairness.

A decade after I graduated, I was asked to come back
to my high school and give a speech. The irony of my
addressing the students at a school where I had not long
before been such a colossal underachiever was certainly
not lost on me. And so as the day of the speech rolled
around, I began thinking long and hard about that
passage from *The Kite Runner*. I wanted very much to
impress the students, to tell them that I had been a hard
worker in high school and that they, too, should dedi-
cate themselves to their studies.

But by that time I had finally come to realize the folly
in pretending to be something I'm not. I knew how dangerous it could be to foster an unreal image of myself,
to accept credit for things I have not done. I knew that
Khaled Hosseini was exactly right: When we tell a lie we
are stealing someone's right to the truth. When we cheat
we are stealing someone's right to fairness.

I knew that I had spent all of middle school and high
school and college lying to everyone, constantly pretending to be someone I wasn't. That's what trying to
get suspended and to be a rebel was all about; it's why

I pretended to be a math genius and claimed to be in the National Honor Society. I also knew that very few people get the opportunity to go back and make good on the situations they got wrong. Most important, I knew I would regret it for the rest of my life if I didn't face the truth when I had the chance.

So when I finished my speech that day, I concluded by calling my English teacher to the stage. When she made it to the front, I reached in my pocket and pulled out the gold shawl I had stolen from her so many years before. I went on to explain to the entire school that I hadn't deserved to be in the National Honor Society. That I had spent the majority of my time in high school being a liar and a cheater. That it was time I stopped stealing. That it was time I gave the school some truth and fairness.

As I left the school after my speech, I remembered the day I had pulled away from the same parking lot feeling like a math genius. Then I thought about the day I had peeled away after having been suspended. And while on this day I didn't leave the school feeling cool or intellectual, I left feeling something better.

I left feeling honest.

Man-to-Man Chats

In the beginning was my grandfather. And the word was with my grandfather. And the word *was* my grandfather. A strapping mountain of a man, his name was Dr. Cyrus Leighton Gray. He was the first radiologist in my hometown of High Point, and because of this I thought him more brilliant than Einstein.

Not only was he a Duke Med grad, but he was also the quintessential Southern man. He chewed Red Man tobacco and drove a beat-up Chevy Silverado. He listened to Willie Nelson and Johnny Cash and went on fishing trips to places like Montana and Idaho. He taught me how to cast a rod and how to fire a gun, how to wedge my bubble gum against my lower lip so it would bulge out like a plug of tobacco. He also showed me resourceful things: things like how to keep a canned drink cold while fishing (by lodging it between rocks in the coolest waters of the stream) and how to evade eating my vegetables (by slipping them onto his plate while my mother wasn't looking).

I considered everything my grandfather did or said a work of wonder. This is likely the reason why, to this day, I find the word *damn* so pleasing to the ear and why I believe Willie Nelson is and will always be the best candidate for president of the United States.

One of my earliest memories is of sitting in my grandfather's den, on a tiny wicker chair, studying him as he towered over me in his burgundy leather recliner. The fire beside us made the gray stubble on his face glow red. I was about five years old, and we were having what he liked to call a "man-to-man chat."

During these talks, I would drink Coke from a Donald Duck sippy cup and watch my grandfather's every move: the way his knuckles bulged as he gripped his highball glass (which I later found out contained a healthy portion of gin and OJ), the way his whole body shook when I made him laugh, the way his eyes went distant when I'd ask pressing questions about my deceased grandmother.

We had these man-to-man chats nearly every afternoon, when my mom would take me to see him after he got off work. We would discuss all the really pressing issues in society: soccer games, T-ball games, Disney movies, etc.

But on the afternoon I remember most vividly, my grandfather got really serious with me—something he had never done before. His eyes narrowed as he considered me. Finally, he took a deep breath. "Austin, will you make me a promise?"

I nodded.

"Will you promise me that when you grow up, you will never sell yourself short?" He paused, as if searching for the right words. "That you'll always do what *you* want to do?"

I looked at him uncertainly.

My grandfather's face turned pensive, as if dissatisfied with his question. His jaw muscles tightened, and his eyes stared past me. I could tell he was wrestling with wanting to ask me something else. After what seemed like minutes, he looked back at me.

"Will you make me another promise?" he said.

Again I nodded.

"Will you promise me that when you grow up you will believe in someone bigger than yourself?"

I was five years old, and I had no clue what he was talking about. I said, "You mean like a *six*-year-old?"

A big, toothy grin spread across his face. He leaned forward and patted my head. In a voice scarcely above a whisper, he said, "One day, son. One day you'll understand what I mean."

A little over two years later, my grandfather had a heart attack. I sat in the emergency room experiencing a feeling of helplessness I'd never known. It was a pivotal moment in my life. I was suddenly facing one of life's most painful realities: just because you love someone doesn't mean he or she will be around forever.

A couple of hours later, word came back that my grandfather was stable. After my mother explained to me that "stable" meant that he was going to survive, I sat in the waiting room with my head bowed, relieved in spirit but unable to regain the childish innocence I'd had only hours before, the feeling that had let me believe that everything would be all right.

Three days later, my grandfather was released into my mother's care. He needed twenty-four-hour supervision, so he had to move into my parents' house. Our house was very small, and we didn't have a guest bedroom. So my mother turned our living room into a makeshift bedroom for him, and when he got there, he found not just one bed in the room but two. I had pulled my own little bed in there and positioned it right beside his.

I watched him nap that first day. I sat upright and still on my bed, my legs tucked tight to my chest. I had resolved that I would sit beside my grandfather and beat the death away, and if I couldn't, I would be right beside him so he wouldn't feel alone when he left for heaven.

For the next couple of weeks I slept in the living room, and I remember most everything about those nights: the way the traffic noise was louder than in my bedroom, the way the wooden floors groaned in the middle of the night as I stumbled for the bathroom, the way *Murder, She Wrote* came on the TV each night at nine, because my grandfather liked that program.

My parents worried about me in those weeks. They wondered why a young boy would rather watch an old man sleep than go outside and play. What my parents didn't understand was that there was more going on than a boy sitting at his grandfather's bedside. They didn't realize I was beginning to grapple with the big issues.

I was chewing on everything I'd been told about life and about death, running the equations, and trying to piece together all the information I had on God and heaven and angels and Jesus.

It was the first time I'd ever felt the need to call on God for anything. I began praying fervently that God would make my grandfather healthy again, that one day soon he'd be the same person I used to know: the virile man who used to take me fishing and hunting, the man with whom I used to sit by the fire and drink Coca-Cola and have man-to-man chats.

I prayed long.

I prayed hard.

In the end, my grandfather lived a little over a year longer, though he was never quite the same. He could barely walk. He could barely hear. Wet spots would seep through his sweatpants around his crotch, his urine coming out blue because of the pills he was taking.

Finally, he conceded to cancer on June 1, 1991.

As I sat at the funeral crying, wondering how I was ever going to make it through life without my grandfather, I thought about those man-to-man chats and remembered the promises I'd made him.

On my season of *Survivor*, the sixteen contestants were organized into tribes like this: four older men, four younger men, four older women, four younger women. When looking to cast the "young men's" tribe (that's really what they called us), I'm pretty sure the show's producers scoured the entire United States in search of the four most inept, unprepared young men they could find.

And rest assured, they found us.

My "young men's" tribe was stranded on the island for nearly seventy-two hours and had yet to make a fire—even though we got flint on the *first* day. Looking back, I think we were under the impression that having flint was like having a garage door opener: that we'd just point it at the kindling and, poof, we'd have fire.

Suffice it to say that using flint isn't so easy.

We four morons spent three full days huddled over broken twigs, cracked tree branches, torn clothing, and anything else we figured might be flammable. By the middle of that third day, our flint had been whittled down to a nub.

Meanwhile we were trying to build a shelter. The one tool we were given was a machete; with that in hand we set off to work. And since we were, in fact, young males, we tackled this task in the manner most befitting our sex: we pretended to know what we were doing and tried to out-testosterone one another. By the third day we had collected enough bamboo rods and palm fronds to build a wall that could secure our nation's border. With adequate material gathered, we moved on to the construction phase.

This turned out to be a highly elaborate process: we took our bamboo rods and, in what can only be called an "inspired" move, leaned them against one another. Then we tentatively affixed the palm fronds for roofing.

Looking back on what we built, it is safe to say we erected the worst structure in architectural history. It wouldn't have withstood a spitting competition, let alone a rainstorm. Now, we were doing all of this work under a Panamanian summer sun that must've had the temperature up to 150 degrees. But we had no fresh water; we had to make a fire so we could boil the seawater and make it palatable. When my legs began involuntarily quaking, I knew I was getting seriously dehydrated—which scared me.

I remember dropping my machete and walking to the beach. Staring across the ocean, I mumbled something like this: "All right, God, I know the Bible says you will supply all my needs, so I believe that. I really do. I guess I don't *need* water right now. I guess I just want it. But when it comes time that I need it, I'd really appreciate you hooking me up. Because I'm getting awfully thirsty out here."

After I finished my prayer I sat down for a while, letting the sand run between my fingers like a five-year-old. I sat like that for several minutes, trying to think of a way to skirt manual labor without being conspicuously absent. Realizing this was impossible, I grudgingly walked back up to camp.

About an hour later I was "working" on the shelter with one of the guys when I heard a shriek of joy somewhere behind me. I wheeled around and saw two of the guys jumping around like we'd just won an immunity challenge.

Apparently, I had become so used to the sound of machete on flint that I didn't realize the other two were still trying to get fire. But sure enough they had produced a baby flame. The four of us spent the next hour on our knees, huffing and puffing on that little flame, trying to make it rise (for those of you keeping score, oxygen is a component of fire building). Finally, panting like we'd just completed a marathon, we were standing over a full-blown fire. We boiled a pot of water and drank our fill.

A couple of hours later one of the producers called me aside for an interview, and one of her first questions was why I had walked down to the ocean by myself earlier. I responded by saying that I'd just had "one of the most awesome spiritual moments I've ever had."

Unsurprisingly, the producer looked at me the way Matt Lauer looked at Tom Cruise when he got going about Scientology on the *Today* show.

Consequently, I stumbled through my words, but here's what I wanted to say to her:

I'm not one of those Christians who believes that if I pray hard enough for something God's going to grant me my wish. Nor do I believe that we were able to make a fire that day simply because I said a prayer. Instead I learned something very important about faith through that prayer.

Though I'm not always a model Christian, I've kept the faith for a long time. I've prayed many times in my life. But when I finished praying that day, it occurred to me for the first time that I really did believe I was talking to somebody. In other words, I found out that I really did believe that there was someone bigger than me out there, someone all-powerful and all-loving, someone who really *was* listening to what I had to say.

At that point I learned a beautiful truth about life: it is such a blessing to believe in someone bigger than myself.

Eighteen days later, a girl named Danielle and I got banished to what was known as Exile Island. Being sent to an island all by yourself, without food or shelter, is a pretty big bummer to begin with, but when God recreates Noah's Flood while you're there, it's a real drag. In other words, Danielle and I were on our own for nearly thirty-six hours, and it rained the entire time.

And I'm not just talking about rain.

I'm talking about a deluge, maelstrom, monsoon. I'm talking about the kind of blinding downpour that makes you pull onto the shoulder if it starts coming down while you're driving. The kind movie characters walk around in just after getting dumped.

Twenty-four hours into the experience, I was ready to break. The isolation I felt was sobering and intense. All across the ocean lightning cut the sky while thunder boomed, deep and steady. As the storm raged on, I sat curled in a fetal position, trying to maintain as much body heat as possible. The show's producers, wrapped snugly in Columbia rain gear, instructed us on signs to look for in case hypothermia started setting in.

I had been praying incessantly since the rain began.

But as the storm persisted I began to wonder if my prayers were going unheard.

I felt an unfamiliar bitterness slowly seeping through me. It is a terrifying moment for a Christian when he realizes that he is beginning to question whether God is really listening.

If God were real, I began telling myself, if he was, in fact, the loving, benevolent Father I'd always believed him to be, then he'd be keenly aware of how close I was to my breaking point. I'd been earnestly calling on him for help for over twenty-four hours, and I had been met with zero response.

I felt my spirit giving way and my emotions taking over.

My first curses came out scarcely above a whisper. As time went on, they became confident sentences. Soon I was screaming curses at both the weather and God, not at all unlike Lieutenant Dan when he and Forrest Gump were abandoned at sea amid a monsoon.

For the next few hours I rode a roller coaster of emotions. I went from screaming to praying to cursing to praying again, from begging God to make the storm stop to thanking Him for putting me through such a difficult trial, and back to cursing, to screaming, to praying.

I'm not going to lie to you: throughout those miserable hours I considered quitting. I considered it hard.

But when the morning sun slowly began to climb above the horizon, and I pulled off my soaking wet shirt after nearly thirty hours of misery and felt the heat slowly melt away the goose bumps on my arms, I finally knew why I was on *Survivor*.

I realized in that moment that *Survivor* is not just a game show. I realized that *Survivor* is not just an opportunity to win a million dollars.

I realized that *Survivor* is a microcosm of life.

Survivor is about pushing each contestant's back against a wall, about pushing him into a place he's never been before and never wanted to go, a place where he wants to quit. But, just like in life, he knows he can't quit, that quitting is for cowards.

And so he's forced to fight.

And then he's forced to pray.

And then he's forced to *doubt*.

And then, finally, he's forced to believe.

And when the storm clears, he comes to find that if he believes in himself, he can do a whole heck of a lot.

But he also finds that if he believes in someone bigger than himself, he can do *anything*.

As I stood there that morning on Exile Island, looking over the Atlantic Ocean and watching pale blue skies chase away the storm clouds, I found myself thinking of my grandfather and remembering those promises I made to him all those years ago.

My grandfather knew what I, in my childish innocence, did not. He knew that life is hard. That it's unfair.

That it kicks your butt and bloodies your lip and seldom explains why. And most importantly, he knew how much easier life can be when we break down if we really *do* believe in someone bigger than ourselves.

So for a brief moment, it was as if my grandfather and I were together on a tiny island somewhere off the coast of Panama, having a man-to-man chat. The only things missing were the wicker chair, the Donald Duck sippy cup, and a healthy dose of gin and orange juice.

Thanks, God. Bye!

Today's sunshine was pretty. Thanks, God. Bye!

The epigraph above was the ending of a prayer I once heard made by a five-year-old girl. I've come to believe it to be the most selfless, beautiful, profound prayer I've ever heard.

Several years ago, a group of single guys and I used to hold a Bible-study session every Tuesday night. It started out with four guys getting together to discuss a few ideas about the Christian faith. Eventually, it snowballed into a weekly shindig where as many as ten guys would show up. On certain nights we'd have vulnerable, in-depth discussions where we'd be real with one another about our struggles and fears. We also had many unproductive nights during which everyone seemed more concerned with appearing religious than tackling substantive ideas. Either way, no matter what direction our conversations took, we always began by saying a prayer together.

One Tuesday, one of my buddies was praying and I heard him do something I had lately noticed many Christians (especially me) do when praying: he kept readdressing Jesus by name as he prayed. I remember him saying something like, "Jesus, thank you for this chance to come together. We pray, Jesus, that you'd be glorified. Jesus, we ask your guidance tonight, and we thank you, Jesus, for . . ."

I remember several years ago being at a Bible-study session where the teacher causally mentioned that Abraham was the only man God ever called his friend. Days later, that statement came back to me. My train of thought went exactly like this: First, I was awestruck by Abraham receiving such an honor—I mean, really, how cool would it be for God, the Creator of the Universe, to call you his "friend"? Then I began wondering if I was God's friend. It occurred to me that I was probably Jesus's friend, since I believed in him, but I doubted this logic was supported anywhere in the Bible.

I happened to be on my way home to read a book as this was playing out in my head. By the time I got to my room, I was still so moved by the idea of being God's friend that I decided to read my Bible instead. With no specific direction in mind, I grabbed my King James and began flipping, ultimately deciding to read something printed in red. I settled for the first red-covered page I came to and began reading directly where my eyes fell.

The passage I landed on was from John 15, and the first words I read were: "You are now my friends."

I nearly jumped out of my chair. Looking back, I figure the odds of my turning directly to that passage, in that moment, have to be roughly three million to one. No bookie would handle a bet like that.

Ever since that day, I have slowly been realizing that Jesus is not just my God, not just some all-powerful deity, but also, and perhaps more importantly, he is my *friend*.

This brings me back to my main point.

I have a best friend named Robbie, and I am so comfortable with our friendship that I can call him whenever and just start rambling. Now, let's imagine I called Robbie up and said, "Hey, Robbie, I was just wondering what you're up to, Robbie. Are you planning on doing anything tonight, Robbie? Robbie, I think we should go grab a beer, Robbie."

Robbie, after most likely getting annoyed, would ask me why I kept saying his name over and over.

The point, of course, is that when you are truly someone's friend, all pretenses and formalities get thrown out. And if Jesus is in fact our friend, then shouldn't we view him that way? I fully believe that we are to revere God, that we are to love him and fear him, but aren't we called to be his Son's friends, too?

The term *friend* hints at fun, at playfulness—at being

comfortable. And I know, for my part, I've spent far too long being stoic and stiff with God.

The more I thought about it, the more I realized I was too full of polished religious lingo. My prayers mirrored the one my friend made that Tuesday night at Bible study. I was talking with God as if I had no idea who or where he is.

I think Martina McBride stumbled onto something with her song "God's Will." The song is about her constant longing for truth and peace and how she finally found them through observing the innocence of a terminally ill boy named Will.

I wish I could have the faith and understanding of a child, because children are so much wiser than we are. I am finally beginning to understand why the Bible says, "Except you become like small children you will not enter the kingdom of heaven."

I believe that the kingdom of heaven is not just this notion we have of the afterlife, not just this image our minds have created of streaming waters and peaceful meadows. I certainly think it's more than just a movie starring Orlando Bloom. I believe that the kingdom of heaven also includes the wide expanse of love and communion we have with Jesus right here, right now, if we're willing to address God like that adorable five-year-old girl did: like he's our friend.

Going forward, I have one simple goal when it comes

to praying, and that is to consult with Jesus as if he's my best friend. I want to laugh with him, cry with him, and, most important, I want to stop saying his name so many times in order to convince myself that he's really out there and listening. I already know where he is: he's in my heart and he's all around me.

Thanks to the realization I had that night at the Tuesday Bible-study group, I have taken a whole new approach to my prayer life, and my zeal for Jesus has increased exponentially. The steps I've taken are very simple, yet they have enabled me to really get to know Jesus as my friend.

I left Bible study that night unable to get the words, "Thanks, God. Bye!" out of my head. No matter what else I tried to think about, those three words haunted me. So as I drove home that night I found myself turning down the volume of the radio and beginning to talk to Jesus. Only, this time I was doing just that: I was *talking*.

I said, "Hey, Jesus. I don't really know what I'm doing right now, but I'm going to try to talk to you like I would a real person. I mean, I believe you when you say that I'm your friend, so from now on I'm going to try to talk to you that way. I hope you don't mind, but I'm going to start talking to you like you're my buddy. I really don't have much else to say other than that right now. But I'll talk to you soon. Thanks, God. Bye."

And as soon as I finished praying, I felt a strong sense of peace. I knew in my heart that I was really talking to Jesus. And for the first time, I felt like I'd said exactly what I wanted to say. There was nothing religious about the prayer. It was simply a running dialogue of what I was thinking that very second.

Five minutes later, I was so excited about this new relationship with Jesus that I wanted to talk to him some more. So I began talking again, saying exactly what came to mind. What I said seemed trivial: I just told him that I really liked the song I was listening to and that I was excited that I could tell him about it. But then, after speaking to him, I realized that because the message was trivial its implication was anything but. It was, instead, eternally significant. I realized for the first time that, because of Jesus's resurrection, the God of the Universe is actually interested in *anything* I have to say to him.

This new discovery set me ablaze, and I began talking with Jesus all the time. I would tell him important things, and I'd tell him simple, trivial things. Each time I felt pleasure knowing that I was consulting with Jesus, that he really cared about what I had to say.

But then bedtime came.

For me bedtime has always been a moment for a more formal prayer. It's almost as if I viewed bedtime prayer as an entrée and other prayers as appetizers: sometimes you have an appetizer and sometimes you don't, but the entrée is a definite.

I geared up for the bedtime prayer, snuggled my head into a comfortable spot on the pillow, closed my eyes, and began to pray in my new method. And as the words left my mouth, I made a shocking discovery.

Since in this prayer forum (bedtime prayer) I discuss things that are very important to me, I do something that many other Christians I've heard pray also do: I keep saying "I pray."

Suddenly, I began wondering whether God really needed me to tell him that I was praying. After thinking about it for a second, I realized that since he is omniscient, he is probably already aware that I am praying, so I decided to cut the term *I pray* out of my prayer.

That's when I made my shocking discovery.

When I consciously tried to stop saying "I pray," I ended up inadvertently substituting the words "I want." And no matter how hard I tried to stop saying "I want," I couldn't do it. It was too ingrained in my system of prayer.

I found that I was rationalizing my neediness by hiding behind the words *I pray*. When I said what I really mean, the same phrase came out "I want."

For instance, my prayer might sound something like this: "Jesus, I pray that you'll give me a peaceful night sleep. I pray that you'll bless my writing and I pray that you'll bless my family."

Taking out the words "I pray," that prayer would sound like this: "Jesus, I want you to give me a peaceful night sleep. I want you to bless my writing and I want you to bless my family."

Isn't this remarkable?

For the first time, I saw myself as painfully needy. No matter how hard I tried to stop, I couldn't prevent myself from telling Jesus what I wanted Him to do for me. It occurred to me that if Jesus is really my friend, then we aren't having a very bilateral relationship.

And, to top it all off, I found that I was ending my prayers like many people I've heard pray, saying, "And I'll give you all the glory. Amen."

I had to laugh out loud at the absurdity of this. Essentially, my prayers were nothing more than a list of what I wanted God to do for me. And then, at the end of this list, I would promise God I'd give him all the praise if he'd just give me what I wanted. This would be like me asking Robbie to run to the store and pick me up a Gatorade and Snickers, head to Blockbuster to pick up a movie, pop the flick in the DVD player, and throw me the remote, and then saying I would be willing to acknowledge him for doing it. Some trade-off.

Of course there is a difference between asking Robbie for something and asking for favors from God, but, still, aren't they both supposed to be my friends? I have a hunch God has grown very tired of me doing nothing but asking him for things.

There is a Christian writer I greatly admire named Watchman Nee. Nee says that a proper prayer should not be, "Lord, I want," but instead, "Lord, thou art." Lately, I have been giving this some serious thought.

I'm beginning to realize that Jesus would like to hear me tell him how great he is from time to time, how he would like to hear from me more often than when I want to talk about myself. I'm realizing that he would like me to ask how he's doing from time to time. And by that I mean that he would like me to point out all of the amazing things about him. He'd like me to reflect on the wonders and mysteries of nature and praise him for his creativity. By doing these things, by lending voice to our belief that he is all-powerful, we are in essence saying, "Lord, you created all of this. How did you do it? How did that *feel*?"

And subconsciously our spirits are nurtured, because Jesus loves for us to give him praise, to give him acclaim. Sure we need to ask God for things, we need to seek him for guidance and blessings, but when it becomes our only reason for prayer, we're turning a beautiful friendship into a unilateral arrangement.

I will never forget the epiphany I experienced as I lay in bed that night and stared at the ceiling, thankful there was no mirror nearby to show me what the face of selfishness looked like. I resolved from that night forward to stop constantly telling Jesus that I was praying, because he knew what I was doing. I wasn't praying, I was *requesting*.

Jesus saved my prayer life. Quite literally, he saved it. He turned a practice I was bored with into something exciting and fresh. Today I talk with Jesus the same way that five-year-old girl did, by saying exactly what's on my mind and then telling him that I'll talk to him again soon.

The Love Boat

Not long ago I was asked to speak on a Christian music cruise. It turned out to be a really neat event that featured something like twenty-five major-label Christian bands, a half-dozen renowned Christian speakers, a couple of renowned Christian comedians, a renowned Christian magician, and me. Technically, I was also a speaker, but since I was not "renowned," I didn't count myself as falling into the same category as the others. I viewed myself as my own entity on the ship, a stand-alone, an independent—the Ross Perot figure, if you will.

I was slated as the "Singles Speaker," which meant that I was responsible for addressing the unmarried folks on the cruise. I thought this made a lot of sense, seeing as I was, in fact, unmarried. I did wonder whether it would be a problem that I didn't believe in "kissing dating good-bye" like so many other young Christians, but it turns out that offering a pro-dating message to group of twentysomethings who all want to get married and settle down is a bit like pushing Justin Timberlake tickets at a sorority car wash.

The trip lasted four days and took us down to Jamaica and back. I was allowed to bring a friend and, since I *was* unmarried, and since bringing along a girlfriend to share your bunk is somewhat frowned upon at Christian events, I elected to take Chris.

We had a great time relaxing in the sun and listening to lots of music. However, what I remember most about the cruise is not the music or the fun but an interaction I had with a woman on the ship's deck.

It was nighttime, on the second day of the cruise, when this woman approached me. Chris had just left in search of soft-serve ice cream, so I was standing alone, listening to a band called Sonic Flood, watching the group's lead singer bring the set to a close. I felt a tap on my shoulder.

"You're the guy from *Survivor*, right?" said a voice behind me. Turning, I found myself facing a very tall woman with dark, curly hair.

"Yes," I said, dragging the word out like the guy in those old Bud Light commercials.

"Yeah, you spoke at the singles' session this morning, didn't you?"

I shrugged. "Well, I guess that depends on whether you like what you heard or not."

The woman smiled. "Oh, I didn't make it down there. I was busy with another commitment. But I had planned on it."

"Well in that case, then yes, I spoke this morning at the singles' session."

The woman extended her hand and introduced herself. "I have not watched much *Survivor*, to be perfectly honest with you. But it is a real pleasure meeting you."

"Likewise," I said.

"I hope that doesn't offend you—that I don't watch your show. It's just that I find it to be so immoral, you know? What with all those people out there just using each other to advance themselves. Lying, cheating, stealing . . . I just can't bring myself to watch it."

I smiled. "Don't worry; you're not the first person to tell me that."

"So how *did* you deal with it?" she asked. "I mean, obviously you did, because you're here right now. How did you manage to keep your Christian witness in the face of all that temptation?"

This is a question that I still, to this day, get asked very often in Christian circles, and I don't know that I totally understand it. Because I don't know that I really acted much differently from the people on the show who weren't Christians. The only real difference between them and me was that they didn't believe in Jesus while they were starving, and I did.

"I guess I just tried to do what I thought was right," I said simply. "But trust me, I told a couple of lies and did some things I'm not proud of, too. So I don't know that I can really accept any compliments about maintaining my Christian witness."

"Well," the woman said, "I just think it's so fantastic that a young man your age is willing to stand up and represent the Lord the way you're doing."

"Again," I said, "I really don't know whether I deserve that kind of compliment, but I appreciate you saying it."

The woman shook her head and sighed. "I just wish my daughter could have been here to hear you speak."

"Oh yeah?" I said. "Why's that?'

The woman scratched her head. "She's just gotten into all sorts of sin lately. I don't know . . . it's just . . ."

I stood and waited for the woman to continue. Ultimately, she went on to tell me that her daughter had been smoking weed and sleeping around while away at college. She told me that she believed this was happening because the girl had not gone to church in quite a while. She said that she often pressed her daughter to find a church at school and start going, but the girl would respond by rolling her eyes and making snide comments.

I remained silent for a minute, thinking. Finally, I asked if she thought the root of the problem might be deeper than just absences from church.

"What do you mean?" she said.

"Well, it's just that I have been down similar roads myself, and if your daughter is anything like me, she probably just wants to feel accepted and secure."

I went on to suggest that the deeper issue could be an identity thing, that the girl thought partying and hooking up with guys would make her feel more important and give her something to share with the other coeds.

"It's my experience that those things in and of themselves don't fully deliver," I said. "So maybe your daughter will soon feel that way, too. Maybe that will be what points her to Jesus."

"Go on," she said.

"In other words, maybe it is less about her church attendance and more about how she is defining herself."

The woman stiffened, and I quickly sensed that something I said had not landed well. "I don't agree," she said. "Sure, college kids want to fit in with the crowd, but I don't see how encouraging my child to go to church can have anything but a positive effect on her. Hearing God's word each week is the only thing that will bring change."

I opened my mouth to respond, but the woman checked her watch and told me she was running late to meet her husband. She politely scurried off, leaving me dismayed. I felt awful that she had gotten the wrong impression, because of course I believe that going to church and engaging in Christian community is transformative. Nothing is more special to me than being able to enjoy Jesus with like-minded people. It's just that, from personal experience, I know that church isn't especially beneficial if you haven't really established an identity in Jesus. And I suspected that this was the real issue her daughter was facing.

That night I thought about the girl quite a bit, wondering whether she was like so many other young adults who have confided in me in the last few years. Was she scared of judgment at church? Did she believe the church wouldn't understand what was going on inside her head: her concerns and motivations? Did church seem intimidating and unapproachable? I wondered if she was just like me at her age, if she had heard a lot about Jesus at church but didn't yet have an idea of who he really is.

To this day I often reflect on that girl, because to me she is representative of all the people frantically searching for meaning but put off by church and religion. As I travel the country, people frequently tell me similar stories. They tell me how bored they are with church, how they are numb to religious platitudes like "Just give it to the Lord" or "I'll be praying for you." They say it all sounds good but doesn't actually *mean* anything to them. They say there is no substance behind it.

From personal experience, I understand where they are coming from.

I think we are all filled with inordinate amounts of fear and envy and longing. We're all searching for meaning in a fast-paced, increasingly global community and trying our best to appear to have everything together. Many of us have mortgages and spiffy cars we can't afford, just to look like we make more money than we really do. We post pictures of our spouses (or significant others) on our MySpace pages and write biographies for our Internet communities about how "happy" we are, just to project a false image of prosperity and happiness.

But I believe that we all sense there is something else, something missing, something we want. So we hop from bed to bed, do drugs, get hammered, buy expensive things. And when those things don't deliver, many of us finally look to church. But if religion doesn't quickly fill the void, we move on to something else. It's almost like we approach church with a mentality that says, "Okay, God, my life is in shambles right now and I need a quick fix. So if you'll help me out, I'll believe in you and keep coming. But if this doesn't work within a week or two, I'm moving on to something else."

At least that's how I always approached it.

It took me years of searching before I realized that, in going to church simply to seek a quick fix for my problems, I was overlooking the deeper issue—the one I was trying to explain to the woman on the ship. I finally saw that my *reason* for going to church had to be more important than the actual practice of going. I had to understand that religion wouldn't deliver unless I knew who I really was and what I really wanted. In other words, I had to be humble and broken, in need of redemption, finally able to admit that my life was a stage play, that behind the curtain I was hanging on by a thin thread. I had to accept that all the external things I was doing, like buying a newer, bigger car or wearing designer jeans or climbing the social ladder or giving money to a church, were simply attempts to avoid facing my fears and insecurities.

I had to make some important concessions about myself, to myself. I had to acknowledge that:

I don't have much money.

I'm *terrified* of people not liking me.

I'm not nearly as smart as I want to appear to be.

I'm scared to death of not being in control.

The list goes on.

Until recently, I did everything I could to hide these insecurities. I tried to convince everyone how successful I was as a writer, even though all I had ever done was self-publish a novel. I borrowed my parents' BMW to go on dates so that girls would think I was making lots of money. I lined my bookshelves with copies of big books like *War and Peace* and *The Odyssey* (neither of which I'd ever read, and still haven't) because I thought they made me look smart. I wore nice clothes because

I thought they made me look trendy. I learned how to play Dave Matthews Band songs on my guitar because I thought knowing those songs made my guitar playing seem cool.

I never allowed anyone to meet the real me; they only met my representative.

Meanwhile, amid all my personal insecurities, I had another, bigger identity crisis going on: I was torn between my understanding of Christian faith and my questions about what I was really doing here, what my *purpose* was. I went back and forth between strictly adhering to biblical morality and living a worldly lifestyle.

I went through spurts during which I attended church fanatically because I wanted so badly to be a devout Christian; I wanted to share with others the ideas that the church told me would make me feel rewarded. But simply going to church and trying to be a "good Christian" did not fulfill me at all. In fact it made me feel even emptier, because it made me feel unqualified to be a Christian. Each time I would go back to church, I would find myself intimidated by the whole idea of religion. I'd start thinking that I didn't possess the innate goodness it took be a "real Christian." I wondered if maybe, given the various sins of my past, I was already too far gone. Feeling this way, I would soon stop going to church and immediately begin seeking fulfillment down the same old avenues: alcohol, sex, money, the pursuit of material possessions. None of it fulfilled me. I couldn't overcome the pressing feeling that in reality my life was hollow, that it was nothing more than a show.

Then one autumn morning, after waking up hung-over in some stranger's bed, feeling disgusted, knowing I couldn't keep living this way, I finally turned to Jesus—not to church, but to Jesus. Feeling so small, so broken, so in need of redemption, I opened my Bible and started reading the Gospels for myself, trying to figure out who Jesus really was, to find out what he really stood for. And what I found surprised me. I found that Jesus was the type of realist I had always professed to want to be. I learned that he was loving and patient and that he was the type of God who didn't require his followers to be perfect; instead he *expected* his followers to be flawed and shameful. I realized that Jesus was the type of guy who was full of integrity, the type who wouldn't take crap from anybody. At the same time, he was inviting and approachable; he was the man everyone confided in and looked to for guidance. Then I read about Jesus blamelessly hanging on a tree just so that *any* human being, when tired and hollow and broken, could call on him, too; they could confide in him and look to him for guidance.

I realized that there was a vast gulf separating the

Jesus I was reading about and the "Christianity" I had experienced most of my life. Suddenly, Jesus seemed so much more appealing to me, so much more approachable. He was so much better than the two-dimensional, judgmental God I had always imagined him being, so much easier to relate to and engage with. It was on that day that I really fell in love with Jesus, and for the first time, the following Sunday, I went to church because I really *wanted* to.

When I look back on my own experience with Christianity, I see that somewhere along the way I turned God into some sort of lifestyle coach, one who would make me run laps and do push-ups every time I fumbled the ball. It's as if I never wanted to go to practice because I didn't understand the game.

It is my experience that if you don't feel like you know Jesus, church is intimidating. It seems like everyone in the building is looking right through you, that they are all judging you and thinking you're full of crap. Feeling like an outsider at church is not really any different from feeling like an outsider among peers or in society. There's no real difference between feeling foolish in a fraternity for being a virgin and feeling foolish in a church for not being able to find Philemon in the Bible. Both situations make you feel left out and insecure. That's why understanding the difference between going to church and knowing Jesus is so important—if Jesus isn't the reason for being there, then church is just another social club, a boring one with strict rules.

So when people tell me that they don't like church, that they find it boring, I reply that they are in good company. I suggest they read the Gospels for themselves, see what Jesus was really like. I tell them they might find, like I did, the hope his message was intended to convey—how he stood for humble love in a cruel world and how he promised us that by loving him we could have redemption from our insecurity and emptiness.

Baseball and the Rhythm of Life

I thought I was done with baseball.

My Chicago Cubs will never win the series, I don't drink much anymore (which makes going to local minor league games somewhat pointless), and I haven't played in over a decade. Until recently, I was convinced there was nothing left to tie me to the game I used to love.

Then the phone rang at six one dark Monday morning.

"He's gone," were the barely distinguishable words that came through the other end of the line.

I didn't need to hear more, because even though the only sound that followed was sobbing, I knew what had happened. After a two-month struggle with cancer, my best friend Chris's father, Rev. Bruce Hopper, had gone to be with his best friend, Jesus.

As I hung up the phone and rose from my bed, desperately hoping to wake from a nightmare, I was hit with the full effect of what I'd just heard. The man was gone; he was gone and he was never coming back.

I began to cry.

Bruce Hopper was a man of integrity. When life tried to beat him down, he would explain in his thick Southern drawl that matters of this life aren't eternally important. And he'd *mean* it.

Bruce was a dynamite preacher who was offered pastoral positions at numerous large churches throughout the South but turned them all down (along with the larger income they would have provided) because he loved his little flock in High Point. Bruce was a throwback to an older generation of preachers. If he had lived in Andy Griffith's Mayberry, he would have preached on Sunday mornings and then headed over to the jail to drink Coca-Cola with Otis, showing the drunkard, by the example of his own spirit and behavior, how Jesus is a stronger medicine than gin.

Chris once told me how, in a time of personal despair, he had been making late-night trips to a small lake in High Point called Oak Hollow. He was in a rut, having been hurt by someone he cared about very much. For several nights he had been going out to the lake by himself, telling no one that he was spending his evenings on an otherwise empty dock, staring into the winter sky and quietly asking the stars questions about life and God and love and heartache. But one night, he heard the dock creaking. When he turned around, he found that his father had followed him. With a Bible in hand, Bruce sat down beside Chris. Just as he had when Chris was a child, Bruce waited for his son to express his concerns. When Chris said nothing, Bruce began talking.

Not about God. Not about heaven. Not about anything clichéd one would expect a pastor to discuss with a hurting son.

Instead Bruce talked about life, about his own experiences dealing with the difficulties of young adulthood, about the tough realities of heartache. And while the Bible was with him the whole night, Bruce never gave Chris a sermon. Instead the book sat unopened in his lap, coloring everything Bruce said with love and affection. And when they left the dock together, Chris felt, for the first time in weeks, a measure of hope. Bruce had spoken to his son the ultimate words of God, without once having to mention his name: he'd shown the boy unconditional love.

Several days after I learned that Bruce had cancer, I was eating lunch with my mother at Carter Brothers Barbecue (a staple for good Carolina barbecue here in High Point).

I remember looking up from my hush puppies and seeing Bruce walk through the bell-jingling door. I told my mother that I wanted to talk to him, but that I didn't know what to say. In typical fashion, I was making the situation about myself. I knew that having a conversation about his cancer would make me uncomfortable, and I wanted to avoid the situation like a frightened five-year-old.

But seeing as I had known him for over fifteen years and his son was my best friend, courtesy won out and my mother and I went over to say hello. When Bruce looked up from his green beans and saw us standing before him, he beamed with a smile more purposeful than I'd ever seen. A glow surrounded him so deep and true I wouldn't have been shocked if he had suddenly sprouted wings and started strumming a harp.

After a few long moments of small talk, Bruce finally addressed the elephant in the room. And instead of bemoaning his plight, he told us a story that I later recounted to anyone who'd listen to me.

Bruce told us that when he first heard his prognosis he hit rock bottom, that all his wife, Doretta, could do was hold him as they both wept. But as the days went by, he began considering his life, replaying his fifty years, and, finally, resigning himself to his diagnosis. He figured that if Jesus was ready to call him home, then he'd be waiting at the bus stop with his bags packed and a smile on his face.

Bruce said that several days after accepting that he was going to die, he was sitting in his rocking chair on his front porch, thinking back on his life, thanking God for his many blessings, and, for the third time in his life, he felt God speak directly to him. Bruce said he felt God whispering in his spirit, saying that the cancer was nothing for him, that he could rid Bruce of his cancer in an instant, that he had a much bigger plan for everything.

After Bruce told us this, he went on to say that he had no doubt God would heal him. He fully believed this. So did his wife and children. So did every one of his parishioners.

So did I.

In the wake of Bruce's passing, many questions were left unanswered: Where was God? Why would God allow this to happen? If God really spoke to Bruce and told him he'd heal him, then why didn't he?

There was a time when I would have pretended to have an answer for questions like these, a time when I would have tried to paint a glossy finish over the canvas of someone else's pain and loss.

Well, here's what I believe now: There *is* no answer. There is only the promise of faith; nothing more.

In scripture faith is defined as "the substance of things hoped for, the evidence of things unseen." In light of a tragedy like Bruce's, one can only cling to faith when seeking an answer for the tears.

There are many who think those of us who lean on faith are fools. And I'll admit, at times I understand their reasoning; yet I still choose to believe.

Everyone in Bruce's church was braced for a miracle. It hadn't crossed anyone's mind that Bruce would not be healed and would not be preaching again by the end of the year. His passing was devastating. But on the Tuesday morning following his death, the sign in front of Bruce's church read, "We *Still* Believe God Heals."

So far as I can determine, there is no particular reason why God chooses to heal some people and not others. I have witnessed and heard of miracles beyond explanation. I have also watched my uncle, one of the greatest men I've ever known, die of cancer before reaching fifty years old. Why some and not others?

There is no reason; only faith.

Lately, I have grown dismayed by the way I see many Christians respond in situations like these. In moments of tragedy or embarrassment or confusion, it seems our response has often been to cover everything up, to pretend like we have an answer, to smile and pretend like we aren't hurting.

But here's what I've found out: People are flawed. Everyone has moments of doubt. Everyone hurts.

Jesus, the man responsible for our faith, taught us that

life is unfair. He taught us that life is hard, that we are all going to experience tragedy. And before he died, he reminded us that if we simply believe in him throughout our misfortunes, then we will see him again someday.

He never promised us that we'd be perfect. He never promised us that if we believed in him we would have "happy" lives. Most important, he never promised us that it would be easy to believe.

But he did say that we'd have peace. He did say that we'd be fulfilled.

At her husband's funeral, Doretta Hopper's face showed us the truth of these promises. As Bruce's best friend concluded his eulogy, saying, "My friend Bruce Hopper is now in heaven," Doretta, with tears in her eyes, nodded her head and smiled. Despite her sadness, she had found the ultimate peace one can have in this world: she knew for certain that the person she most loved was where he wanted to be.

Bruce's passing reminded me why I'm a Christian. It reminded me why I have accepted the idea that I don't have to understand all of life's mysteries.

It also reminded me why I love baseball.

As Bruce's brother Curtis spoke to the congregation and remembered the big brother he idolized as a boy, he spoke of how great a pitcher Bruce was. He told the audience something many of them never knew: Bruce had once had a very good shot at being a professional baseball player but quit the game to become a preacher.

As I sat in bed crying that Monday morning after receiving the call from Chris, I remembered the first time we'd met, at the High Point Little League ballpark. We played catch together. On that dark morning, knowing there was nothing I could say to cheer Chris up, knowing there was nothing I could do to fill the void of his father's passing, I decided to find my old ball glove and ask him to play catch.

As we stood in the cul-de-sac in front of his parents' house, quietly tossing a baseball back and forth, I watched Chris's delivery, the fluidity with which he threw the ball to me. I reflected on the hundreds of games during which I had stood in center field watching Chris go into a windup, knowing the batter was doomed. I thought about Bruce teaching Chris to throw a baseball, about Bruce's own father teaching him to do the same.

That day, watching the purity of Chris's throw, its effortless grace, I was struck by how much better than me he could throw the ball. It didn't make much sense, because we had grown up playing together. We had the same coaches and the same instruction. But then it occurred to me: there is no rhyme or reason for why some people are good pitchers and some aren't. In that moment I understood that while the mechanics of throwing—just like the substance of faith—can be taught, in the end, a true gift is something one either has or doesn't have. It is something within us, something that can never be formulized or acquired through practice. It was Bruce's DNA working inside him that enabled Chris to be a good pitcher; just as I believe it is God's own DNA working inside all of us, enabling us to persist in our faith even when it can't be explained.

Likewise, it's not just baseball skill that Bruce gave to Chris but everything he loved and stood for. It's rocking chairs on breezy afternoons and Carter Brothers Barbecue; it's Sun-Drop soda and humility; it's smiling when there's no reason to be happy and laughing when there's no humor. But chiefly, it is loving Jesus Christ even when there's no understanding his reasoning.

Bruce loved the New York Yankees. For whatever reason, he adored that pin-striped money machine. And though he never got to touch the green grass of Yankee Stadium or shake hands with George Steinbrenner, he received a gift far superior. That dark Monday morning, as I hung up my telephone, a tall left-handed pitcher with a thick Southern accent walked the golden streets of heaven and looked into the eyes of an almighty God. Bruce heard those words that all of us who share his faith long to hear: "Well done, my good and faithful servant."

While there will never be answers for why he left us so early, those of us who remain will press on with the faith that we don't need them. We will follow Bruce's lead. We will throw on our gloves and trot out for the next inning, fully aware that anything could happen next and that we need not worry about the reason why these things unfold.

I can close my eyes and imagine a day in the future when, if Chris and I are blessed with sons of our own, we will stand around a grill in his backyard and watch them play catch. When that day comes, I'll watch Chris's son begin his windup, and as he releases the ball, I'll remember anew what faith is all about.

Acknowledgments

Somewhere, some aspiring writer is looking through this book *just* to read the acknowledgments page. You see, as aspiring writers, this is what we do. So, if the aspiring writer in question happens to be *you*, I say this: Keep with it. Persevere. Don't let the fear and doubt overcome you. Then, I say this (because I know it's what you really want to know): My agents are Mary Beth Chappell and Jennifer Gates at Zachary Shuster Harmsworth. As such, they are the first people who deserve my thanks.

MB: Where to begin? You are my friend, my ally, my sounding board, my fellow hunter of white whales. You not only made my dream of being a published writer come true, you also kept me sane along the way. A simple "thank you" doesn't cut it. I am forever in your debt.

Jenn: Thank you so much for plucking my query from your slush pile, calling me, listening carefully, and then agreeing to represent me. I always feel like I'm at home when I visit you in New York. I look forward to a long career of working together.

Not only did my dream editor, Carolyn Carlson, read

my proposal, she actually agreed to take on the project. Then, once Carolyn worked her magic on my words, she called in her associate, the brilliant and hilarious Kevin Doughten, to work his.

Carolyn, only in my wildest dreams did I imagine having an editor like you. Your direction, encouragement, enthusiasm, and, perhaps most important, your genuine warmth, are what enabled me to write this book. I am forever grateful that you took this chance on me.

Kevin, you turned my wayward ramblings into clear and cohesive thoughts. You are not only the wittiest and funniest dude in publishing, but, in my opinion, the young buck with the most promising future. It has been my pleasure to work with you.

Special thanks go to Cherise Fisher, editor in chief at Plume, who believed in this project from the beginning. Thank you, Cherise!

These people at Plume also deserve my thanks: publicist Liz Keenan and production editor Lavina Lee. Thank you to copy editor Ted Gachot, as well.

Koren Zailckas, you provided me encouragement and guidance and sanity and inspiration. Thank you for all of it . . . and then some.

Michele Ambrosino, manager of the High Point Barnes and Noble, granted me my first book signing when I was twenty-one, broke, and struggling to hock a self-published book. Michele, I will never forget that you were the first person to say yes.

Thank you Mom and Dad, for loving me and believing in me and encouraging me. I love you both beyond measure.

And the same goes to you, Elizabeth. You are the sweetest, most caring person I know, and I am so proud to be your big brother.

Grandpa, it was you who told me about Jesus when I was little and then showed me who Jesus was as I got older. And if ever you needed reinforcement, Grandma, you were right there behind him. You're the strongest woman I know (and I mean that quite literally: You are eighty-seven and still lifting weights). I love you both, and hope that you are proud of this book and its message.

Jeff and Leann Spencer were kind enough to loan me their beach house for five days so I could knock out a chunk of this book. However, because Ocean Isle, North Carolina, is so beautiful, I didn't write a single word (literally, not *one*). But, thank you, Jeff and Leann, all the same.

Special thanks go to my buddy Ryan Miles, who contributed in several different ways to this project.

These people all read drafts of the book (some of them numerous times). Their suggestions were invaluable and I am indebted to them all. They are: Jane Stephens, Matt Schneider, Ed Piacentino, and Greg Farrand.

Thank you to Wes Yoder and the whole gang at Ambassador.

I would be remiss not to thank Erika Shay, Lynne Spillman, and Mark Burnett for voting me into the tribe.

To all of my friends who appeared in this book: Thank you for sharing your life with me and for allowing me to share it with others. And for my friends who don't appear in this book: I'm grateful for all of you (and watch out, I may ask to share your stories in another book).

This book simply could not have been written were it not for April Nicholson. Not only is she the love of my life, she's also my unofficial editor. Ape, you listened to me, encouraged me, counseled me, and loved me through this whole process. You read every word at least five times . . . then you kindly (and patiently) told me how to make each one better. I was a lost, selfish little boy until you came along. Thank you for making me a better man. I love you.

(*I know, I know . . . begin cueing the "play off" music . . .*)

Other than my apartment, this book was written in three places: the Starbucks on highway 68, the Starbucks at the High Point Barnes and Noble, and Black Bear Coffee in Hendersonville, North Carolina. Thank you to the employees of each of these establishments for your kindness and support and free refills.

To you, reader, I extend my profound thanks for taking the time to read along. It really does mean the world to me. I would love to hear your thoughts and opinions on my thoughts and opinions (oh, and even if you hated this book, how about telling everyone you know to go buy a copy?). You can e-mail me directly at austincartybook@gmail.com. I'll be on the lookout for you.

Finally, I wish to thank God for creating my story, Jesus for writing its resolution, and, not to be forgotten, their loving Spirit for allowing me to write the plotlines in between.